MW00873798

Spiritually Single Wives

Kathy ~

Thank you
for being my "girlfriend",
I could not do life without
your friendship in quite
the same way! :)

Chris

Spiritually Single Wives

For Christian Women

Who Share Everything with Their Husbands...

Except Their Faith

Chris Moss

SSW Publishing

San Diego, California

SSW Publishing

http://www.SpirituallySingleWives.com

© 2010 by Chris Moss

Library of Congress Cataloguing-In-Publication Data

Moss, Chris

Spiritually Single Wives: For Christian Women Who Share Everything With Their Husbands... Except Their Faith /

Chris Moss

Includes bibliographic references.

1. Spouses—Religious life. 2. Marriage—Religious aspects—Christianity. 3. Spiritual Life—Christianity.

Printed in the United States of America

10　9　8　7　6　5　4　3　1

First edition

All rights reserved. Printed in the United States of America. No part of this book may be used or reproduced, in whole or in part, in any manner whatsoever, including display on the Internet, without written permission from the author, except in the case of brief quotations with attribution, embodied in critical articles and reviews.

Limits of Liability and Disclaimer of Warranty. The author and publisher shall not be liable for the use or misuse of material contained herein. This book is strictly for informational, educational, and entertainment purposes only.

This book is dedicated to the two loves of my life:

Jesus Christ and Ed Moss.

May the words on these pages bless you both!

CONTENTS

Introduction

My husband is the love of my life. I absolutely adore him. I say this without apologizing for my choice to marry a Jewish man, even though I had been a Christian for over 20 years at the time.
Yes, I chose to be unequally yoked. Yes, I rebelled. Yes, I have repented and yes, I am forgiven.

I lived for years feeling sorry for myself: sitting alone at church and explaining why I was always in a hurry to leave. I seldom made commitments and when I did, I always felt conflicted or flakey. I realized later in my marriage that my choice to marry a man who does not share my faith lead to bigger and bigger compromises. I was lonely, frustrated, and envious of others with Christian husbands.

But I believed in love. I believed in the love that Ed and I shared, and I believed in the redemptive love of God. So I asked God, "Is there no redemption?" Be careful what you ask God because the lessons keep unfolding! It started with 1 Peter 3 — and not the part about the wives married to unbelievers. If you've been married half a minute, someone has already burned that into soft places. But this:

> Finally, all of you, live in harmony with one another; be sympathetic, love as brothers, be compassionate and humble. Do not repay evil with evil or insult with insult, but with blessing,

because to this you were called so that you may inherit a blessing. For, whoever would love life and see good days must keep his tongue from evil and his lips from deceitful speech. He must turn from evil and do good; he must seek peace and pursue it. For the eyes of the Lord are on the righteous and his ears are attentive to their prayer...

1 Peter 3:8-12

After reading this verse, I looked at the rocky time we were going through, I turned heavenward, and I said to God: "So what about my blessing! Just because I married a Jewish guy, I don't get a blessing? Come on! You chose the whole Jewish race! I just chose one! Lord, give me a break! I know I was called for more than conflict in my marriage. I want my blessing! What do I have to do to live in your favor?"

The result of that initial confrontation with God began to unfold through the years. It was rough at first, but the result has been freedom, peace, joy, love, and contentment. Now many of the same exercises that God took me through are written on the pages of this book for you. This book can be used in various ways. It can be a quick and easy read for your personal spiritual growth and motivation. You can also read it in a book club with other women. There is a study guide in the back of the book that will allow you to lead a small group of spiritually single wives. Choose what you need and grow! There is tons of help on my website: www.spirituallysinglewives.com.

I want to take a moment to thank my spiritual partner Donna who has been my prayerful support for years. I am proud that she is my spiritually single friend and has kept me on track. Thank you also to Lori Naseef and the spiritually single wives at Kensington Community Church in Troy, Michigan where this material was born and where I was privileged to co-lead a small group. I want to thank Linda Hoover and

Gwen Schakett at Calvary Community Church in Westlake Village, California who believed so much in this material that they allowed me to teach it. And thanks to all the women of Westlake Village, Thousand Oaks, and the many places I have had the privilege to be involved with who have read and provided comments to help me improve the delivery of the material, prayed for me, and for this book. I truly believe this book is delivered to you on the power of their prayers.

One more thing: Ed has never read a page of this book — even though this is his story as much as mine. He knows it is written to an audience he will never be a part of: Christian women. If you ever meet him, pretend you don't know him — even though you will know him quite well by the time you have finished this book.

When it became time to title the book, Ed's suggestion was "The Christian and the Yid!" I keep him around for many good reasons, but one is because he makes me laugh. Feed your sense of humor. It's one of the best attributes of spiritually single wives!

Blessings!
Chris Moss

One

Spiritually Single

'For I know the plans I have for you,'
declares the LORD,
'plans to prosper you and not to harm you,
plans to give you hope and a future.'

JEREMIAH 29:11

What Is Spiritually Single?

The first time I heard the term *spiritually single* it hit me like one of those enormous wave curls in the ocean that crash over you when you least expect it. I even gasped a little like I'd been splashed, but this time the splash was a new understanding. Two little words that when put together finally described the condition of my life: spiritually single.

I mulled it over for days and I just kept feeling that wave wash over me (and tasting sand). Before I knew I was spiritually single, I had the feeling that I was being pulled under by something, and I could not quite put my finger on it. I got sucked into sadness and depression. But once I understood what *spiritually single* meant, I began a new journey in life.

It's like this: When I am at the beach and a wave knocks me down, I get up, dry off and make a decision about my next move. Am I going to jump back into the ocean and let it make sand out of me again? Or am I going to learn a lesson and either finesse the next wave or go back to the shore and wait? I applied this analogy to my life. I decided to dry myself off and start a new journey. I did not know where it would lead, but God knew. It was my choice to obey and follow Him.

I am a happily married woman who shares nearly everything with a great husband. Ed and I do everything together; we love to share the same food, music, sports, people, and politics. Everything, except Jesus. In the early years of our marriage, this did not seem like such a big difference, but we serve a jealous God who wants our focus. As I changed and became more willing to surrender to Jesus, my husband continued marching down our previous path; he remained the same. As Jesus began to permeate and stabilize some of the lifelong messes I had made, Ed saw the change in me. He readily admits that he has benefited from some of the changes. But some of the external change — out on Sunday mornings and Wednesday nights, crying through episodes of grace and forgiveness, ridiculous hopefulness even in the darkest situation and the celebrations of seemingly minor victories — were harder for him to grasp.

For a while, Ed thought I was a wreck! He thought I had temporary insanity. But most of all, he thought if he just waited it out, I'd move on to something else. It's been years and my husband is still waiting. I usually attend services alone, pray alone, and do my devotions alone. I very rarely have the opportunity for an intimate spiritual discussion with the man with whom I share my life, my everything. Sometimes it's lonely.

I realize today that we may get lonely, but we are not alone. There are many spiritually single women, and you may be one of them. We just need to find each other. We all have unique circumstances, but we all became spiritually single by God's grace — yes really, by his grace! God did not slap his forehead when you chose your husband and grumble, "What could she be thinking!?" He knew your choice long before you were born and he has walked ahead of you to prepare every step. This man is in your life to bring out the godly character that God sees in you through Jesus.

The spiritually single can be divided into five groups:

Two prenuptial nonbelievers. Those who courted and married as nonbelievers, one met Jesus later and had a life changing experience that left one mate wondering about the other! If this describes you, your husband may have questioned your judgment, your sanity, or even your future together.

Christians with a low, but compatible, commitment to God. Those ladies who spent a period of their life when Jesus wasn't so important, met a great guy, fell in love, and ended up married to someone who had a limited faith in Christ. Then you met and fell in love with a great God, evolved into a committed follower of Christ, and your husband has not. How does that work?

The Rebel. Those who had a personal relationship with Christ and knew the powerful teachings about being unequally yoked, but got married anyway. You fell in love with a man who was so "nice" or so perfect in all other ways that you knew he would eventually accept the Lord — all he needed was a wonderful partner like you in his life to make the path apparent. Apparently not.

Postnuptial change. After courtship and marriage, your husband left his faith in Christ. He either deceived you about his faith during courtship or had a life change. Whether abrupt or gradual, after the nuptials, life has changed from your original plan and it hurts.

Spiritual imbalance. A married couple that experiences occasional differences in their commitment to Jesus and who feel unbalanced in their walk as a couple. Some event or series of events gets them "out of sync."

No matter how we got here, we don't have to be lonely. We need to stick together. We need to build a community of supportive, encouraging, God-seeking women who will love one another, encourage one another, and pray for one another. Many of us have been lonely or felt like we did not belong for so long that belonging somewhere might be very healing.

Am I Spiritually Single?

Because most women go through periods — even if they are brief — when their walk with God seems to be alone and not alongside their partner, you may want to complete the Self-Rating Scale below. Rate each of the six questions on a scale of 0 to 5, with 5 being strongly agree and 0 being strongly disagree. Then add together all the numbers you selected.

Self-Rating Scale

1. My husband knows Christ as his personal savior.　　　5 4 3 2 1 0

2. My husband lives out Christ-like qualities in our home.　　　5 4 3 2 1 0

3. My husband knows about and respects my decision to follow Christ.　　　5 4 3 2 1 0

4. My husband supports me and our family in our spiritual pursuits.   5 4 3 2 1 0

5. My husband engages in church service on a regular basis.   5 4 3 2 1 0

6. My husband would never make fun of or mock me for my beliefs in Christ.   5 4 3 2 1 0

If you rate yourself at 20 or below on the scale, you are probably experiencing occasional frustration or loneliness associated with being spiritually single. If you have a total score below 12, you probably experience that frustration daily.

In some churches, admitting a low score on this scale might be considered spiritual or social suicide. In the church Jesus loves, I believe a low score is the beginning of wisdom. We may have a harder path, but the good news is that Jesus knew where your path was headed even before you were born. Did we have a choice? Of course we did. Since this is the choice we made, however, God is merciful to meet us where we are.

If you have been rebellious, guess what? Jesus stretched out his arms, died for your sins, and offers you forgiveness. If your husband has deceived you or abandoned his agreement to live in a Christ-centered home, God offers forgiveness for those sins. If Jesus can pay the price and forgive him, shouldn't you extend at least as much grace? And forgive him for what his deception has meant in your life?

Therefore, there is now no condemnation for those who are in Christ Jesus,

because through Christ Jesus the law of
the Spirit of life set me free from the law
of sin and death.

Romans 8:1-2

Did we miss God's plan for our lives? Satan is our enemy and he will use whatever weakness you have to prevent you from reflecting the love of God to your husband. Our enemy would have you believe that you screwed up, chose the wrong guy, and unless he changes you should needle, bug, badger, and cajole until he accepts Christ as his personal savior. If you have tried this, you already know it doesn't work! Another lie is that you should leave him and find someone more spiritually compatible. You may already see behavior patterns in your marriage that suggest that the enemy is alive and using you to judge, condemn, or abandon your husband to salvation. But nothing could be more ineffective or further from the truth!

'For I know the plans I have for you,'
declares the Lord, 'plans to prosper you
and not to harm you, plans to give you
hope and a future. Then you will call
upon me and come and pray to me, and
I will listen to you. You will seek me and
find me when you seek me with all your
heart. I will be found by you,' declares
the Lord, 'and will bring you back from
captivity.'

Jeremiah 29:11-14

Could the marriage partner you chose be the divine plan God designed just for your spiritual growth? Your path with an unsaved husband will provide you with unique opportunities for personal growth you never dreamed of. Your husband has the opportunity to see and experience Christ through you. It is an awesome and rewarding challenge. Your mission everyday for the rest of your life is right in your own home. While others raise money and travel to do missionary work, you can do it at home; sometimes, even in your bunny slippers! And sometimes in your birthday suit (more on that later).

How Does Being Spiritually Single Affect Us?

From a spiritual standpoint, we will not have a marriage partnership when it comes to God. We will not experience shared intimacy about spiritual thoughts with our husbands. They will not encourage us to grow. We will learn to store information like camels to share with our female friends or small group, but we will rarely have the daily interaction with our partners that would feed our souls.

There are times I feel depressed because the flow of the Holy Spirit can become stifled at our house. I go to church by myself and socially sometimes it would just be easier to stay at home than to walk in and sit alone again. Other times I have created a conflict, dragged my husband along to a church-sponsored event and regretted every minute of it. As a woman who is spiritually single, I long to connect with others and need an environment that is safe and supportive to do so. Most times it will not include my husband. When he comes, it changes the dynamics of the worship. I am always more concerned about his thoughts instead of true worship.

Maybe you are a woman who carries guilt for your choice in partners, or you struggle with your heart being held captive by a man who does not cherish Jesus like you do. I know that in my marriage, sometimes it's hard to tell if I love God or my husband more. I really love Ed, and it is often easier to worship him than God. It is always easier to follow him than God — an extra hour cuddling under the warm covers with my husband on a cold, snowy Sunday morning is hard to resist. This behavior is, in a sense, a type of idolatry and one of God's biggest pet peeves about humans (remember the first commandment?). The problem with idolizing Ed is that he will eventually disappoint me. He is not God. We worship God because he never fails us. Who, then, is more worthy of my worship? I believe part of God's plan for the spiritually single is to get beyond the guilt and the idolatry, because we cannot be an example if we are weighed down. We cannot be free to worship while guilt has a foothold in our lives.

"Life would be so much easier if only he was saved," was my mantra for a long time. "If he'd go to church with me and serve God with me — think how much more we could do to make a difference in this world!" That sounds good on the surface, but for me this is just a mask of insecurity. When I make that statement, I want my husband along to validate me and make my life easier, not because I am concerned for his salvation. Nor am I concerned that I, alone, could be doing "more." What am I doing with what I have been given? Our lives should not be made more picture-perfect, but more godly. We should be looking for God's plan and get in on it. I am convinced that God's plan for me was to learn the godly behavior that springs up involuntarily from my satisfied soul through my spiritually single situation. When I know all I need to know at this stage, God will take me to the next challenge. He may send the Holy Spirit to take the veil off my husband's face so that he can be saved. Or not.

It is my genuine hope that through the pages of this book you will find the freedom that Christ offers us no matter to whom you are married and what his beliefs are. It is also my prayerful hope that you will offer your husband that same freedom. I pray that this book will provide you with an opportunity to find out about God's plan for you and the tools you need to connect with other women in a nurturing, healthy environment — to be accepted and loved for who you are. Equally important for us as spiritually single wives is, without ever uttering a word, to reflect that freedom at home so our husbands can be won over by our behavior.

The Next Wave

Go before God and through confession and repentance, cleanse yourself from any sin. (If we confess our sins, he is faithful and just and will forgive us our sins and purify us from all unrighteousness. 1 John 1:9) God knew the condition of your heart when you married, so if you rebelled, ask God's forgiveness now. If you were foolish, ask God to sustain you with wisdom. Praise God for who He is. Focus on His magnificence. Quote scripture or worship through music. Don't rush…enjoy His presence.

Picture your husband in your mind. Visualize him at this moment. See the darkness engulfing him. That darkness is his sin — it keeps him separated from God. Watch in your mind's eye as he participates in the things he does that are a reflection of his unsaved state. Describe it to God verbally. Tell God about his condition. Is he sick? Lonely? Depressed? Doubtful? Anxious? Addicted? Stubborn? Prideful?

Ask God to give you wisdom to pray for your husband.

In the same way, the Spirit helps us in our weakness. We do not know what we ought to pray for, but the Spirit himself intercedes for us with groans that words cannot express. And he who searches our hearts knows the mind of the Spirit, because the Spirit intercedes for the saints in accordance with God's will.

Romans 8:26-27

Imagine now, Jesus reaching out to your husband. Concentrate on Jesus' light. Watch it penetrate that darkness around your husband's sin — erasing it with His dazzling brilliance. Picture your husband moving toward God's light and love. Commit your husband to the Lord —ask Him to shed His light and love on your husband today. Ask Him to woo and minister to him today through the Holy Spirit.

Now, in your mind's eye, give your husband to God. Envision Jesus wrapping up your husband in His arms and completely submerging him in His light and love. Ask God to perform a mighty work in your hubby's life. Ask God to change him into the person He wants him to be.

Mentally commit your husband to being right there in the arms of Jesus from now on. Every time you pray from now on, think of your husband as being inundated with the person of Christ, as what he can become in Him, rather than how he exists in his present state.[1]

We Need Girlfriends

As **iron sharpens iron**,

so one [wo]man **sharpens** another.

PROVERBS 27:17

Who Is Your Best Friend? Why?

As spiritually single women, we may feel lonely in our marriages, unable to share our true selves, our spiritual selves, with our husbands. It is especially important for us to have Christian friends, especially girlfriends who can pray with us and offer support. Friends can share in our joy of being part of God's family, and can help us to grow in our relationship with Jesus.

Donna

Donna walked in late to the first day of our ladies' small group/Bible study. We introduced ourselves around the table and I was the only one who mentioned that my husband did not share my faith. In retrospect, I realize that announcing in a new group that you are married to a nonbeliever could be a social calamity; so very few women are open about it.

Because I was willing to be candid, Donna sought me out after the meeting to tell me her husband was not a believer either. Donna's husband is Muslim and mine is Jewish, which could be a story all by itself. Both are professionals. We both have resources, and we both share a love for Christ and our husbands. Neither of our husbands understands our commitment to Jesus.

It was easy to relate to Donna and I loved her right away. Because of our choice of mates, we both felt like we had one foot "in the world" and one in the spirit. We were often considered too "carnal" for some church activities and way too holy for the nonbelievers we knew.

What do I mean by *in the world*? This phrase is common in Christian circles. It is based on the King James version of John 8:23 where Jesus says he is "not of this world." It basically means Jesus came from heaven and follows a different code. If we follow Him, we choose to abandon our "world" and its code and live by the same code as Jesus did. Spiritually single wives often feel pressure to conform in Christian circles, but if we do, we will not fit in at home.

I use the term *carnal* meaning that we engage in activities from the code of the world. Other Christians may not engage in these activities. Many of us go to Las Vegas. We may gamble or drink alcohol for fun, but not necessarily over-indulge. We may choose an R-rated movie. Many church circles might find our behavior questionable and we will talk about that in later chapters.

Donna and I prayed together, laughed together, played together, shopped together, talked forever, and learned together. And she makes a fabulous, gourmet margarita! In many ways, Donna became the spiritual partner that my husband could not be. I feel fortunate today that she is still in my corner. We pray for each other often and even though I have moved away, we are still remarkably close spiritual partners.

David

Friends are very important — and it is very important in marriages like ours that our friends be females. With male friends there is too much opportunity for emotional or physical adultery — especially for us women who are spiritually single.

Several years ago, I had an experience in which I was tested with regard to my friendships. I volunteered at a local, faith-based charity where the formerly imprisoned were recruited into a program to mainstream them back into productive lives. It was a marvelous organization, and every day I saw God's transformational power in amazing ways through these folks. My husband and I were new to the community and his job kept him traveling frequently. I had lots of spare time to help. It was here that I met David. He was tall, well-dressed, educated, and brilliant. He was very articulate with the tiniest hint of an Eastern accent and he had a chip on his shoulder that rivaled the Rock of Gibraltar. He was newly released from prison after serving two years.

I had taken on a major project — organizing the charity's first gala — so I stayed busy while I was in the office. David worked as a salesperson in the adjoining store and during the times when there were no customers, he brought his Bible and studied it alone for hours. There was an amazing change that started to take place in David. His anger began to be replaced by contentment and the chip on his shoulder dissolved into an intense care and compassion for the people around him. I came in one day with a myriad of tasks to complete in a hurry and he directed his care towards me. He volunteered to become my assistant for the gala. What a gift from God! I could never have achieved such great results without David. His transformation inspired me to get into the Word of God and dig deeper. I began to see God changing me too, making me a new person again after following Jesus for over 30 years!

During the gala season, David continued to work for me like a willing servant. He was the perfect example of the kind of wife I should be! He was such a blessing: praying for me, listening to me, sharing the Word of God with me, listening to Christian music, and taking on every task "heartily, as unto the Lord." He prayed openly for me and always asked for follow-up on subsequent visits. His prayers made him suddenly very....attractive. Yikes! Eventually, I confessed to him that as a wife with an unbelieving spouse, I was concerned with the appropriateness of our friendship, or worse yet, what Satan could do with both our lives and friendship if we were not careful. We agreed that we must be above reproach. After that, he brought an assistant.

After the gala, a series of events transpired and my husband and I moved out of state for him to accept a new job, but our newly renovated home did not sell right away. I wanted to join my husband quickly so I called David to be the caretaker of our home because I trusted him. Before long, David and I were calling to talk frequently about different issues with the house. He shared with me his personal growth and I shared with him mine. By mail, we shared books, CDs, scripture, and the goodness of God. We encouraged one another, loved one another, and became the best of friends.

David provided for me what my unsaved husband could not — spiritual support. Though we were still above reproach via cell phone, I committed what I would call cellular adultery. I couldn't wait for my next talk and the prayer at the end of the call. I finally told him I needed to stop calling him and like a good friend, he finished my sentence, "because our friendship is getting in the way of your primary relationship."

As a spiritually single woman, there is no logical place for a spiritually-intimate relationship with a man to go except to sin. He was a single man with many friends and I was just one of them. He was very understanding, but I grieved the loss of my friend, my spiritual support for weeks after. And after I prayed and thanked God for his intervention, who did I call? Donna! Because she is safe.

> *Be self-controlled and alert. Your enemy the devil prowls around like a roaring lion looking for someone to devour.*
>
> *1 Peter 5:8*

We have an enemy who stalks us like a prowling lion and seeks to destroy us. Our enemy will use attractive, God-fearing men to fill our intimacy-starved souls to lead us to commit sin and destroy us, our marriages, the lives of our male friends, and indirectly our children and the legacy we will leave them. Don't be deceived. We spiritually single wives cannot risk the outcome of an intimate relationship with a male other than our husband.

I knew God had allowed me to experience temptation of biblical proportion. Others in my family had failed in similar situations. I know because I was born an illegitimate child. But when faced with the same temptation, God allowed me an escape of equally biblical proportion through an out-of-state relocation. I had been sifted.

> *I'm throwing Israel into a sieve among all the nations and shaking them good, shaking out all the sin, all the sinners. No real grain will be lost, but all the sinners will be sifted out and thrown away, the people who say, 'Nothing bad will ever happen in our lifetime. It won't even come close.'*
>
> *Amos 9:9-10*

On the other side of that experience has come the blessing of greater intimacy with my husband and a deepening of my commitment to him and to God. My dearest friends came alongside me and listened and encouraged me. I am a stronger person because of that experience.

Spiritual Intimacy

When we are married to an unbelieving man who does not meet our needs spiritually, God's design for us is to become intimately involved with God himself, not another man. I look back at my friendship with David and I realize that just like I used my cell phone to communicate with him while I did my housework, my grocery shopping, my dog walking, I can do that with God. The pattern that evolved as I grew closer to David, I now apply to God. I just keep the chatter going upward and more and more often, I get answers!

So what do we do with our need for human spiritual intimacy? In a word: girlfriends! We need females in our lives who share our needs, like my friend Donna. Females we can trust. Females who encourage and lift us up, and who find us uplifting too.

Every Woman Needs a Mentor

Along these same lines, every spiritually single wife needs a mentor. I have heard the word "femtor" used, which I happen to like better because I think it is more descriptive of women helping women which is critical for our purity. Paul tells us:

> *Likewise, teach the older women to be reverent in the way they live, not to be slanderers or addicted to much wine, but to teach what is good. Then they can train the younger women to love their husbands and children, to be self-controlled and pure, to be busy at home,*

to be kind, and to be subject to their husbands, so that no one will malign the word of God.

Titus 2:3-5

Mentor/femtor relationships do not have to be formal assignments. You may make an informal phone call to one friend regarding an issue about your children. You may check in with another when it comes to an issue about obedience or finances because that person has a successful track record. If you don't experience a long-term connection with someone right away, just continue to pray that God will lead you to your mentor/femtor until you find one or many. Perhaps you have been spiritually single for a long time and it's time for you to share your wisdom with others. After a period of extravagant grace, we reach a dry place if we don't give from our abundance. If you sense that this describes you, there are probably women who are struggling alone who need your help. Pray and ask God to guide you to them.

The Next Wave

WANTED: Spiritually Mature Christian Female. Must be wise, discerning, kindhearted, and savvy. Needed for prayer, encouragement, and guidance. Must have waterproof shoulders to cry on, durable knees for long periods of prayer, and strong backbone to stand up to a friend when necessary. Sense of humor essential. Must be available 24/7. No compensation, but plenty of rewards.[1]

Three

Our Behavior

Wives, in the same way be submissive to your husbands so
that, if any of them do not believe the word, they may be
won over without words by the **behavior** of their wives,
when they see the **purity and reverence** of your lives.

1 PETER 3:1-2

How Do You Feel About the Words Purity and Reverence?

Read these verses from 1 Peter 3 out loud:

> Your beauty should not come from
> outward adornment, such as braided hair
> and the wearing of gold jewelry and fine
> clothes. Instead, it should be that of
> your inner self, the unfading beauty of a
> gentle and quiet spirit, which is of great
> worth in God's sight.

> For this is the way the holy women of
> the past who put their hope in God used
> to make themselves beautiful. They were
> submissive to their own husbands, like

Sarah, who obeyed Abraham and called him her master. You are her daughters if you do what is right and do not give way to fear.

1 Peter 3:3-6

These verses from 1 Peter have been used to beat women up spiritually and to control us through the ages, but that is not what God intended. This verse was meant to be foundational — paramount for the order that God intends in our relationships and for the good of our family and our communities. More on this later.

As a child of the seventies, I have to tell you up front that I am not fond of the words purity or reverence. The world we live in does not consider these virtues today as they were considered when these words were written. But God finds them important enough to have them written for me, a former feminist hippy-type, to find in the twenty-first century. I can't just gloss over them or avoid them. If I am going to follow Christ, I have to be them. That's going to take some significant understanding, so I started with my good friend Webster. Webster's definition for *pure* has four entries that are all included in the Appendix. For our purposes, I chose three definitions that I can learn, live with every day, and demonstrate.

Purity [1] *is the state of being pure.*

Pure [2] *is: 1 free from harshness or roughness and being in tune*

2 a free from what vitiates, weakens, or pollutes; b containing nothing that does not properly belong; c free from moral fault or guilt; d marked by chastity

3 having exactly the talents or skills needed for a particular role

I want to be in tune with my husband. I don't want to make my husband ineffective (vitiate), weaken him, or pollute him. I don't want to hold onto anything that does not belong in our marriage. I don't want to be morally responsible or guilty for anything I do in this or any other relationship. I want to be equipped for my role as the best wife for my husband. In all those definitions, I seek purity. I truly desire to live in "the state of being pure."

Reverence is a bit easier for me. Since the first commercials for the Datsun 240Z, we have built a culture around the word awesome. This word resonates reverence.

> **Reverence**: *honor or respect felt or shown: deference ; especially : profound adoring awed respect* [3]

I really do love my husband and want to adore him. Even at the times when he is least adorable, I want to show him my respect and honor. I just remember how Nancy Reagan looked up at her husband, Ronnie, our 40th President of the United States. She revered him. I think her obvious reverence fed the love between them. I want that in my marriage too, so I will practice reverence. I will find and celebrate his awesome-ness!

If your husband is in one of those "least adorable" stages, ask God to show you how to respect and revere your husband. We don't respect our husbands because they are worthy — they aren't! We respect them because God told us to. As we seek to honor God in our marriages, our respect for our husbands will grow. Ask God to allow you to see the good in your husband as God himself sees the good. Maybe it is in the way he analyzes a situation, or plans his spending or saving. Sometimes it is the way he smiles, sometimes it is his patience, but there is always good because God has created your husband in His own image.

Submission

If we take our definitions and our earlier scripture reference in 1 Peter 3 with Paul's reference to Sarah, it leads us back to Genesis 12. The story of Sarah is an interesting example of submission. Remember when she was Sarai?

> *Now Sarai, Abram's wife, had borne him no children. But she had an Egyptian maidservant named Hagar; so she said to Abram, 'The Lord has kept me from having children. Go, sleep with my maidservant; perhaps I can build a family through her.' Abram agreed to what Sarai said. So after Abram had been living in Canaan ten years, Sarai his wife took her Egyptian maidservant Hagar and gave her to her husband to be his wife. He slept with Hagar, and she conceived. When she knew she was pregnant, she began to despise her mistress.*

> *Then Sarai said to Abram, 'You are responsible for the wrong I am suffering. I put my servant in your arms, and now that she knows she is pregnant, she despises me. May the Lord judge between you and me.'*

> *'Your servant is in your hands,' Abram said. 'Do with her whatever you think best.' Then Sarai mistreated Hagar; so she fled from her. The angel of the LORD*

found Hagar near a spring in the desert;
it was the spring that is beside the road
to Shur. And he said, 'Hagar, servant of
Sarai, where have you come from, and
where are you going? I'm running away
from my mistress Sarai,' she answered.

Genesis 16:1-8

What Happened?

Sarai's lack of faith in God caused her to send Hagar to Abram, creating a child that started a family feud that would cause wars between two nations for generations to come. The pain that the child caused Sarai for years — even after the birth of her own child late in life — was excruciating. It caused her to mistreat her servant. It caused her jealousy and envy. Truly this was not Sarai's finest hour. But God used these circumstances to change Sarai.

So great was the change in Sarai's life that it warrants her mention in 1 Peter. Two times, Sarai followed her husband Abram into foreign lands and protected him by pretending to be his sister instead of his wife. She was taken into the palaces of kings (Genesis 12 and 20) as a royal wife because she supported Abram's lies and God was not happy.

She submitted to living the lie and God protected her while He worked the truth into Abram. By the time she had to participate in this lie for the second time, Sarai was still attractive at age 90.

As Sarai yielded to God and to Abraham, she was truly changed. God blessed her with a new name, Sarah, just as He had blessed Abram with his new name of Abraham.

She was also blessed with a pregnancy and became Isaac's mother in her old age. As the first apostles celebrated Jesus, Sarah gets mentioned because generations later, her humble service resulted in the lineage of Jesus. Hers is a worst-case scenario.

Her story makes me feel so much better about my circumstances. But I want the same blessing that God gave to Sarah.

Let me just go on record on a few points. I have to say honestly, that I would have a really hard time lying to anyone for my husband. And if I did, I don't think I would at age 90 consider pregnancy a reward for supporting my husband in his cowardice and dishonesty. I would be horrified. Palace life would have to be pretty darned incredible for me to support him a second time in the same lie. This little helpmeet would be all over her husband like white on rice for that kind of charade! I would be bitter, angry, and resentful. He'd be making that up to me for a long time! Which brings us to a big question.

Would You Like to Be Married to You?

In Lee and Leslie Strobel's book, *Surviving a Spiritual Mismatch*, they ask this question directly and introduce a concept called "trading up." If I acted out my feelings of anger, resentment, and bitterness for my husband's offenses, would he see Jesus in me? Would he experience the grace of God in our relationship if I continued to exact payment from him?

If you take a long look at the role you play in your marriage, would you want you for a wife? What difference in lifestyle does your husband see in you that makes you and your commitment to God attractive?

> *Jesus said in John 10:10: 'I have come that they may have life, and have it to the full.' When Christians are really living that kind of abundant life — where there's joy, meaning, excitement, purpose, direction, forgiveness, and grace — then their spouse may very well sit up and take notice.* [4]

We hope that our lives reflect something that gets noticed by our spouses in a more positive way.

Trading Up

If you drive a BMW, would you trade it in for a Hyundai? Probably not. So based on your behavior, does a Christian life look like a trade up from the life that your husband is leading? Would he be lured by the abundant life as he looks at you? Is there joy, meaning, purpose, excitement, grace, and forgiveness in large measures happening in your life? Spreading to your family? Would your husband be "trading up" if he bought into what you are living?

As daughters of Sarah, these are the qualities that we want in our lives. We want to be transformed from the inside by Christ, living an abundant life so that all the exterior qualities are a true and attractive reflection of what God is doing in our hearts and minds.

Our behavior must reflect the transformation in our hearts and minds for our husbands to see Jesus in us. Believe me, if you try to fake this, your husband — who knows you better than anyone — will smell hypocrisy before you finish your first attempt at Christian behavior. This is why we must be so dependent upon God. When I realized this, I sensed God was asking me to do something very big and important for my husband: get out of bed. Let me explain.

I am not a morning person. I get up slowly and quietly and as the morning progresses I pick up speed. I pace myself to be ready on time with not a moment to spare. Usually by the time I leave in the morning, I am rushing like a freight train to get one more household task accomplished before I rush madly out the door.

My husband has one pace, not necessarily slow, but very deliberate and purposeful. His pace seldom changes. He gets up and goes through his morning routine and about 45 minutes before he leaves, he sits down in a chair, ready to talk. And I am rushing.

It is nearly impossible to articulate how difficult this is for me. It goes completely against my internal wiring. But God showed me clearly that if I wanted to show my husband I loved him in a real and tangible way that he would relate to, I had to get up and change my most self-indulgent instincts to indulge him instead. I have to be ready to sit for 45 minutes — every morning — and communicate.

As a benefit of my relearned behavior, our best conversations happen during our morning discussions. They have resulted in some intermittent prayers and devotional times that would never have been possible in any other time slot. The intimacy that we share in our early morning talks is unparalleled. The solutions we discover together in these early morning talks are sometimes nearly miraculous. They would not happen if I slept either.

Four Emotional Challenges

If behavior is our key method of communication, and purity and reverence is the goal of our behavior, we need to look at some of the emotional challenges of the spiritually single that often cloud our attempts. Before we concentrate on our behavior, purity or reverence, it will be helpful to look closely at some special pitfalls to which we may be susceptible. Before we were saved, we were flesh. In the process of perfecting our faith, God will allow us to witness our flesh many times in the form of bad behavior. Unfortunately, others will see it too. Perhaps you, your husband, or your kids have even seen a few of these in you.

Loneliness. The more you fall in love with Jesus, the harder it becomes to not share your joy with your soul mate. You want to tell everyone! And you especially want to share the promises, the potential, and the opportunities to serve God with your husband. You want to share with him as you begin to see with new eyes the amazing ways God works. So what happens when he shuts you down? You begin to share less, and the joy that bubbles up inside you becomes loneliness. You may even feel isolated from other believers. This is part of our inherent struggle with Satan's plan to get us alone so he can tell us lies, mistruths, and half truths that will destroy us.

While you feel lonely, your spouse may also feel lonely because the new man in your life — Jesus — brings you joy the way he used to when the two of you first fell in love. He may tire or grow weary of your attachment to a "myth" or a "legend." He may question your stability, your intelligence, or your sanity. He may question whether you are involved in a cult.

Frustration. After a few experiences with your sanity called into question, you may embark on an expedition to prove to your husband that God is real. Though it is very positive and prudent to have loving responses ready for his thoughtful questions, it is not positive to meet him at the door with an arsenal of answers for questions he does not care about. An exercise or two like this leads to frustration for you, as well as your husband. Now he sees his wife, with questionable sanity, actively assaulting him with pride and self-righteousness. Once this threshold has been crossed, it is difficult to recoup, but God is always there to extend forgiveness to you. It will be important for you to confess, repent, and ask for forgiveness from your husband. No matter how hard it is, remember that you are modeling repentance for him in a way that will be very meaningful to him as he comes to know Christ himself.

Expectation. Once you have learned how and when to not talk about Jesus, things drift along well for a while. It is easy to drift into a state of expectation. Sometimes, it swings into full anxiety. You have planted the seeds. You have done the nurturing. You have learned to keep quiet and have nearly bit your tongue off on more than one occasion. You begin to expect God to act. Where are the workers in your mission field? Why can't your husband be blessed with a Saul-to-Paul experience wherein you can witness a miraculous change? Then your husband will become your spiritual partner and he will lead you and your family into a closer walk with God. He will feed the hungry and become a globe-trotting missionary and restore world peace — loved and esteemed for his ability to get things done in Jesus' name. Right?

Have you dared to dream this? Is it wrong to hold onto this kind of expectation? It may not be wrong, but world-wide fame (even in a small way) is full of pitfalls. It limits God to the scope of your dream when His plan for you may be much different and more meaningful to you than even world peace. While you wait in expectation for your good dreams to come true, you may miss some opportunities that are truly great!

In the meantime, while God is working out the details, your home is your ministry. It is your mission field. So while you may not take the mission trip to Africa with your husband to do kingdom work this year, you have the privilege of doing kingdom work in your own home and seeing your husband or your children come one step closer to eternal life. Remember, you are on display at all times as an ambassador for Jesus Christ. Every Christian has a purpose and God-given gifts to accomplish that purpose.

The gifts God gives us connect us to the people of God and will bring us the peace of Christ only when we use them where He intended. That's where the abundant life is. Living in a spiritually single situation, we walk a tightrope. If we lean a little to one side, we avoid stepping out in faith while we wait for our husbands. If we lean too far the other way, we over-step into public ministry and neglect the husbands to whom we have been called to minister.

Church Ladies or Street People?

> *Jesus replied, 'Foxes have holes and birds of the air have nests, but the Son of Man has no place to lay his head.' He said to another man, 'Follow me.' But the man replied, 'Lord, first let me go and bury my father.' Jesus said to him, 'Let the dead bury their own dead, but you go and proclaim the kingdom of God.'*
>
> *Luke 9:58-60*

Just like Jesus, we are between worlds. The people of the temple did not want Him around and the sinners felt uncomfortable with His ability to see them for who they were.

Because we are spiritually single, we may never quite be able to make the social and time commitments of other women we admire at church. We may never fit into the worldly mold that our husbands or their unsaved friends would like us to assume. But that's okay. God loves who we are and where we are.

God can use us in special operations because we can minister to people in informal settings who may never meet Jesus in a church, but might find Him through you on one of your husbands' business trips or outings at a hotel, casino, or a spa. These people would never hear the truth from a man or woman of the cloth, but you might get through their barriers because you look more ordinary, perhaps even approachable. But just watch and be prepared for what

God can do through you because you don't fit in the church or the world!

In the latter part of the above passage, there is another lesson for us as spiritually single wives. "He said to another man, 'Follow me.' But the man replied, 'Lord, first let me go and bury my father.' Jesus said to him, 'Let the dead bury their own dead, but you go and proclaim the kingdom of God.'" One Bible commentary states as follows:

> Though the request seems reasonable, the potential disciple's premise is that family comes before Jesus...As important as taking care of a family member's death is, it is a lower priority.

> Either way, Jesus makes it clear the request should not be honored. Even the 'best excuse' possible should not get in the way of discipleship.[5]

We have to be careful not to use our unsaved husband as an excuse for inactivity.

As spiritually single women, we can spend our lifetimes serving our husbands, waiting for them to become Christians, paying lip service to God and never demonstrating or proclaiming the word of God. This verse exhorts us to proclaim the kingdom of God. There is a myriad of ways for us to give back to God through the body of Christ and find fulfillment without ever encroaching on our partners. It is a tricky balancing act, but when you find a way to give back in the body of Christ, you will find the fulfillment of following God — and the abundant life.

As a spiritually single woman, I served God in ways that would not interrupt my husband or utilize more time than he could understand. I helped with PowerPoint presentations midweek via computer and e-mail without ever infringing on my husband's time. I served in the nursery one Sunday per month during the church service that I usually attended, so it was not extra time away from home on Sunday morning. I served as a Mentor Mom for Mothers of Pre-Schoolers (MOPS) because it took very little prep time and met only bi-weekly — my husband never missed me. I became a pen pal to a prisoner writing a letter of encouragement every two weeks and reading the responses to my husband. He knew I was active, but my activities never encroached on our time together.

Envy. Another emotion that crops up in church circles of the spiritually single is envy. Picture this along with me: You are sitting alone in your usual seat in the sanctuary and you notice a couple about your age, sitting down just between you and the stage. Let's call them Mary and Joseph. They hold hands, laugh at private jokes, and greet friends. They seem so in synch! Their outfits even seem to be color coordinated — did they just step off the page of *Christianity Today*? You know that they had brunch and a family devotional today while you slammed down a half cup of coffee and a stale bagel, then ran out the door hollering at the kids. This is so unfair. Why do you have to sit here alone while Mary and Joseph seem to float together? When will the bump in your bed wake up and complete your dream? Or at least show up so that you don't have to go alone!

Or, picture this: The Saul-to-Paul experience happens, but not to your husband; it happens to your best friend's husband. The friend who sits with you in church every week and has helped you through a million lonely experiences now has a partner in Christ. You have waited in silence serving your man and your God for years, and now she and her husband are embarking on your dream. How will this change affect your friendship? When will you get the blessing she just got? How is that for a distraction? While you want to share her joy, there is an overlay of very human envy.

Envy is a formidable tool of the enemy to prevent us from reveling in the circumstances that God gave us. It is one of the seven deadly sins and Satan can use this one emotion to tear down all that you believe in and have worked for all your life. Confess it to God and allow the Holy Spirit to cleanse you and give you a new perspective — God's perspective. There must be more for you to embark on in your spiritually single journey.

With all these emotions, and there are others, it is very important to take our thoughts captive and remember that God is sovereign and He has a plan that is unique for you.

> *For I know the thoughts and plans that I have for you, says the Lord, thoughts and plans for welfare and peace and not for evil, to give you hope in your final outcome.*
>
> *Jeremiah 29:11 Amplified Bible*

I have gone through seasons when my home was very tense because I was going through a season of one or more of those emotions. There were times I tried to put pressure on my husband to snap to grid, to become the man I thought I needed him to be. My designs and demands were out of line. God knows my situation and created it uniquely and distinctly to bring about my growth and the unique journey He has planned for me. I have to find peace in that. I have to embrace His plan and live that reality out every day. When I resist, I create tension. When I submit, I learn the big lesson: Jesus is not the battleground — He is the prize!

The Next Wave

How would you like to be married to you? Let that be the grid through which you evaluate how you'll react to the ever changing and often disorienting dynamics of a relationship with an unbelieving spouse. Ask yourself that question so often — and wrestle with its implications so honestly — that it begins to reshape your attitude, decisions, and reactions.

The result will be that you will make the most of your spiritual mismatch. [6]

Four

The "S" Word: Submission

Wives, understand and support your husbands in ways that
show your support for Christ. The husband provides
leadership to his wife the way Christ does to his church,
not by domineering but by cherishing. So just as the
church submits to Christ as he exercises such leadership,
wives should likewise submit to their husbands.

EPHESIANS 5:22-24 THE MESSAGE

How Do You Feel When You Hear the Word Submission?

As women of the twenty-first century, the world tells
us it is difficult to believe we are still talking about
submission. Our culture has declared revolt at the very
utterance of the word *submission*. Every women's
magazine out there tells us that we can have it all, that
we just need to "go for it!" Some of us have bought
that. We have gone for it, and we have been successful
at achieving all the world promises. But as Dr. Phil
says, "How's that working for you?" Have you found
happiness? It is a lot of work to be successful in the
world's eyes, and often times in order to achieve
success you have to mow over a lot of people, like
husbands, kids, co-workers, and friends. Once you
have reached your pinnacle, you find yourself alone —

or you find that the bar has been moved, and your pinnacle is still out of reach.

I will be the first to admit that I am a product of my culture. Just like I am not fond of the words *purity* and *reverence*, submission might top my list of things I don't like because it is culturally repulsive. But just like my re-examination of purity and reverence made it relevant and doable, I think the word *submission* might have meanings that we should know, too. So let's re-examine the meaning of submission.

> *Webster's definition of **submission***
>
> *1 a to yield oneself to the authority or will of another: surrender; b to permit oneself to be subjected to something <had to submit to surgery>*
>
> *2 to defer to, or consent, to abide by the opinion or authority of another*
>
> *3 to present or propose to another for review, consideration, or decision[1]*

Submission is an active word that allows us to yield to the authority of another — or to propose for consideration an alternate viewpoint. Taken to its furthest extreme, it can mean surrender — again, an active yielding to the authority of another. Our culture has taken this word and made it ugly to imply that one who submits is acting "like a doormat." Nowhere in the definition does it imply that submission is blind obedience. Submission is not being a doormat; it is not accepting verbal or physical abuse. Submission is not a wrestling match or a series of verbal volleys. It is the give-and-take of two people who care about each other and have each other's best interest at heart.

What Does the Bible Say About Submission?

> *Wives, submit to your husbands as to the Lord. For the husband is the head of the wife as Christ is the head of the church, his body, of which he is the Savior. Now as the church submits to Christ, so also wives should submit to their husbands in everything.*
>
> *Ephesians 5:22-24*

God has lots to say about submission, like the verse we started this chapter with in Ephesians. Another verse I have grown to rely upon to measure my effectiveness as a spiritually single wife is as follows:

> *Be devoted to one another in brotherly love; give preference to one another in honor.*
>
> *Romans 12:10*

According to God, submission is the act of following the prescribed order that He set up for our marriages and our families. Why do we do this? To bless God. Not to be successful, though we probably will know more success if we bless God. Not to please the hubby, because we are human and cannot please even one person all the time. And he will probably be more pleased if your focus is blessing God, because he will experience blessing as a by-product of God's pleasure. Not to affect change in our husband, because we can't change anyone, only the Holy Spirit changes us. We will probably see change, but not until blessing God is our focus. We submit because it is a gift we as wives choose to give. There is nothing doormat-like in choosing to give the gift of respect or deference. How would your husband respond if you acquiesced instead of argued? Without rolling your eyes or sighing like you'd been hit in the solar plexus? If we are truly on one team and have one another's best interest at heart, how can we demonstrate that?

I have been married for 15 years. This is a second marriage for both my husband and me. We learned from the mistakes we made in our first marriages and discovered that a lot of the failure of our first marriages rested squarely on our own shoulders. So when I met Ed (six years after my divorce and nearly five years after his), I knew that he would do things that bothered me, but I would have to extend grace to him to make things work. He is admittedly more mature than me, so he thinks most of what I do is fine, and he seldom complains. Submission for me is not about the little things. It is about accepting the really big things — like moving. In fifteen years, I have moved from my home in California to seven other states, some of them twice, for a total of thirteen moves. My husband is the CEO of a media company and every time he takes on a new challenge and achieves any level of success, an article appears in the trade journals. Invariably, he gets a call from someone with a similar issue who wants to hire him. He has never been unemployed. He has never looked for another job. They just happen for him.

When my husband is considering a new opportunity, the instant he walks in the door before he opens his mouth to tell me about it, I see the look on his face. He loves a good challenge in his profession. The wheels turn, the eyes twinkle, and the creative juices flow. Every time he consults me about the possibility of a move, I tell him my honest opinion. Sometimes we go to the new city, and I tell him I don't like it or I don't want to move there. There have been times when I expressed my opinion and he agreed. Like the time I picked him up from the Orange County Airport (in California) and instead of driving him home, I drove him to the beach with the sun-roof open and the windows down. I begged him through tear-filled eyes, "Please don't make me leave this!" A few weeks later, we were headed to Michigan — in January with snow above my California-bred thighs. My submission at that point was to God, my obedience was to God. I could not stand my husband.

But something happened in Michigan. I went to Michigan out of obedience to God and He met me there. I found the best church I had ever gone to with more opportunity to serve and try out my gifts. That church became the birthplace of this book. I made deep, long lasting friendships with spiritually single wives. I met my friend Donna. And Ed? He went to Michigan for the money. He was lonely and depressed. He had money, which is why he came, but no personal satisfaction or peace.

No matter who you married, when God talks about love and submission it is in the context of Christ's incredible love for the church. Whether or not your husband knows how to love like Jesus does (even Christian men don't know this stuff and have to be taught!), he is worthy of your submission solely on the basis that he's your husband.

God's love compels us as believers to forgive others as we realize how much grace God has already extended to us by sacrificing Jesus on the cross for our sins. Every offense you ever committed is on that cross. Every offense you have ever endured in your marriage — or ever will endure — was paid for on the cross. If Jesus offers forgiveness to your husband, just as he did to you, wouldn't it be at least appropriate for you to offer forgiveness as well? While we lived in Michigan, I forgave Ed for taking me away from the place and people I loved in California (that had to be God, because how else would that be possible?) because my obedience brought me God's tremendous blessing.

Have you ever had a disagreement with your husband over a certain decision and yielded to him only to realize you were right and he was wrong? Every decision has ramifications and sometimes when we submit to our husband, God allows consequences that further develop him as the man he was created to be. The consequences may also strengthen us, encourage us, reinforce previously learned concepts, or teach us something that we could not learn elsewhere. In those instances when you could say "I told you so," I pray that you no longer verbalize it, just thank God that He knows why you are together!

One of the most eye-opening situations I have ever witnessed is when an acquaintance of mine who is in her eighties had a disagreement with her husband of nearly 60 years. He was about to make a real estate deal to move them out of their home and into an active adult community. She was not ready to go. She stated her opinion. He insisted. Before long, my friend consented, the arrangements were made and my friend assisted her husband with his plan. When I asked why she gave in, she had a pearl of wisdom that I have clung to, "I can be right, or I can be married."

Let that sink in. I can be right or I can be married. Sometimes, submission is that simple. If we learn that today, we will be able to operate with the wisdom and experience of a woman married 60 years. We can collect untold blessings with each experience throughout our lifetime with her philosophy.

Everyone must submit himself to the governing authorities, for there is no authority except that which God has established. The authorities that exist have been established by God. Consequently, he who rebels against the authority is rebelling against what God has instituted, and those who do so will bring judgment on themselves.

Romans 13:1-2

Overruled Submission

Let's take a look at an interesting example of submission from the story of Esther. As the first biblical account of a spiritually single wife, Queen Esther was submissive to her husband, the non-Jewish king — except when God overruled it. There was a situation when it became clear to her that the right thing to do was to risk the consequences of not submitting. Read the story from the book of Esther below.

> Mordecai had a cousin named Hadassah, whom he had brought up because she had neither father nor mother. This girl, who was also known as Esther, was lovely in form and features, and Mordecai had taken her as his own daughter when her father and mother died.
>
> When the king's order and edict had been proclaimed, many girls were brought to the citadel of Susa and put under the care of Hegai. Esther also was taken to the king's palace and entrusted to Hegai, who had charge of the harem.
>
> ...And this is how she would go to the king: Anything she wanted was given her to take with her from the harem to the king's palace. In the evening she would go there and in the morning return to another part of the harem to the care of Shaashgaz, the king's eunuch who was in charge of the concubines. She would not return to the king unless he was pleased with her and summoned her by name.
>
> When the turn came for Esther (the girl Mordecai had adopted, the daughter of his uncle Abihail) to go to the king, she asked for nothing other than what Hegai,

the king's eunuch who was in charge of the harem, suggested. And Esther won the favor of everyone who saw her. She was taken to King Xerxes in the royal residence in the tenth month, the month of Tebeth, in the seventh year of his reign.

Now the king was attracted to Esther more than to any of the other women, and she won his favor and approval more than any of the other virgins. So he set a royal crown on her head and made her queen instead of Vashti.

Esther 2:7-8, 13-17

[Mordecai] also gave [Hathach] a copy of the text of the edict for [the Jews'] annihilation, which had been published in Susa, to show to Esther and explain it to her, and he told him to urge her to go into the king's presence to beg for mercy and plead with him for her people.

Hathach went back and reported to Esther what Mordecai had said. Then she instructed him to say to Mordecai, 'All the king's officials and the people of the royal provinces know that for any man or woman who approaches the king in the inner court without being summoned the king has but one law: that he be put to death. The only exception to this is for the king to extend the gold scepter to him and spare his life. But thirty days have passed since I was called to go to the king.'

When Esther's words were reported to Mordecai, he sent back this answer: 'Do not think that because you are in the *king's house you alone of all the Jews will escape. For if you remain silent at this time, relief and deliverance for the Jews will arise from another place, but you and your father's family will perish. And who knows but that you have come to royal position for such a time as this?'*

Then Esther sent this reply to Mordecai: 'Go, gather together all the Jews who are in Susa, and fast for me. Do not eat or drink for three days, night or day. I and my maids will fast as you do. When this is done, I will go to the king, even though it is against the law. And if I perish, I perish.'

So Mordecai went away and carried out all of Esther's instructions. On the third day Esther put on her royal robes and stood in the inner court of the palace, in front of the king's hall. The king was sitting on his royal throne in the hall, facing the entrance. When he saw Queen Esther standing in the court, he was pleased with her and held out to her the gold scepter that was in his hand. So Esther approached and touched the tip of the scepter.

Then the king asked, 'What is it, Queen Esther? What is your request? Even up to half the kingdom, it will be given you.'

Esther 4:8-5:3

'If it pleases the king,' she said, 'and if he regards me with favor and thinks it the right thing to do, and if he is pleased with me, let an order be written overruling the dispatches that Haman son of Hammedatha, the Agagite,

devised and wrote to destroy the Jews in all the king's provinces. For how can I bear to see disaster fall on my people? How can I bear to see the destruction of my family?'

King Xerxes replied to Queen Esther and to Mordecai the Jew, 'Because Haman attacked the Jews, I have given his estate to Esther, and they have hanged him on the gallows. Now write another decree in the king's name in behalf of the Jews as seems best to you, and seal it with the king's signet ring — for no document written in the king's name and sealed with his ring can be revoked.'"

Esther 8:5-8

When Submission Goes Badly

Everyone must learn to submit, to give a gift of lovingly yielding to the order that God has created in our lives. As we learned from the last chapter, godly submission will always reveal purity and reverence. God will never call us to sin in our submission — if he did it would not result in purity. If our husband calls us to sin, then we must submit first to God's call to not sin, and then we can also follow Webster's third definition of submission: "to present or propose to another for review, consideration or decisions"[3] as we pray for our husband's favor and ability to see the truth.

The last word on submission: If you think that you, or someone you know, is in an abusive relationship and has mistakenly called it submission, The National Domestic Violence Hotline is 1-800-799-SAFE (7233) or their website is www.ndvh.org. God never intended our abuse. If you are experiencing abuse, get help now to make it stop.

The Next Wave

I am significant. Life has meaning. There is a higher purpose. I want to believe it, but I may not feel significant until someone expresses love to me. When my spouse lovingly invests time, energy, and effort in me, I believe that I am significant. Without love, I may spend a lifetime in search of significance, self-worth, and security. When I experience love, it impacts all of those needs positively. I am now freed to develop my potential. I am more secure in my self-worth and can now turn my efforts outward instead of being obsessed with my own needs. True love always liberates.[2]

Five

What a Man Wants

Her husband has full confidence in her
and lacks nothing of value.
She brings him good, not harm,
all the days of her life.

PROVERBS 31:11-12

What Do You Think Your Husband Wants From You More Than Anything?

After gaining some understanding about purity and reverence in previous weeks, the best way to put that information into action is to apply it to our marriages. But first, we must try to understand a man's perspective of a "good marriage." He may not be looking for God's design: purity, reverence, and submission in a biblical sense. In fact, he may find them irrelevant; but he is looking for your support. As we understand our non-believing husband's perception of what he needs to achieve a good marriage, we can tailor our actions to support our husbands in meaningful ways. Let's look at some universal imperatives.

Three Things a Husband (Christian or Not) Wants in a Marriage [1]

Respect. When you got married, hopefully you married your best friend. You knew on your wedding day that your love would move mountains and that nothing could or would ever separate you. And a few minutes later, you woke up! Your marriage has been challenged at times and in ways you never dreamed could be possible. But, no matter what, the one thing your husband counts on you for is R-E-S-P-E-C-T. Aretha Franklin sang it, but the lyrics were written by a man: Otis Redding. Your husband needs to know that when everyone in the world challenges him or turns on him, when the going gets tough, when the chips are down, you have his back. You, his best friend, soul mate, life partner and wife, choose to support him. If you remove this key element from your relationship, the rest won't be important enough to sustain you.

In the early church, there was much confusion regarding marriage. Followers of Judaism who had been active participants in the temple were becoming part of a new community of believers leaving behind non-believing spouses. Should a new believer leave his or her spouse if the spouse continues in the old ways? Paul says this to wives:

> *Out of respect for Christ, be courteously reverent to one another. Wives, understand and support your husbands in ways that show your support for Christ. The husband provides leadership to his wife the way Christ does to his church, not by domineering but by cherishing. So just as the church submits to Christ as he exercises such leadership, wives should likewise submit to their husbands.*
>
> *Ephesians 5:21-24*

From the definition we learned in Chapter Four, as Christian women we are called to revere (or respect) and submit (defer to or propose for consideration) to our husbands. The example we are to follow is that of the Church. Have you ever been to a church that did not submit to Christ's love and leading? I have had the experience of seeing that first hand, and although the people were trying very hard to please each other, they missed the mark. They missed it by following an agenda that did not reflect God's purpose. As a result, there were hurt feelings and isolation. People left the fellowship, and lots of things did not get done in a way that honored God. On the other hand, in a church where Christ is revered, needs are met, souls are saved, and lives are changed. If it is my job to function as the church in this relationship, which church do I want to be? I want to be the one revering Christ! This plays out in my marriage as respect for my husband. Not because he is worthy (most times, I have to admit, he is more worthy than most), but because by respecting my husband, I bless and obey God.

The follow-up for husbands is a command to love their wives — and for spiritually single wives, wouldn't this make our world complete?

> *Husbands, go all out in your love for your wives, exactly as Christ did for the church — a love marked by giving, not getting. Christ's love makes the church whole. His words evoke her beauty. Everything He does and says is designed to bring the best out of her, dressing her in dazzling white silk, radiant with holiness. And that is how husbands ought to love their wives. They're really doing themselves a favor — since they're already "one" in marriage. No one abuses his own body, does he? No, he feeds and pampers it.*

That's how Christ treats us, the church, since we are part of his body. And this is why a man leaves father and mother and cherishes his wife. No longer two, they become "one flesh." This is a huge mystery, and I don't pretend to understand it all. What is clearest to me is the way Christ treats the church. And this provides a good picture of how each husband is to treat his wife, loving himself in loving her, and how each wife is to honor [respect] her husband.

Ephesians 5:25-33

The Message

Heavy sigh. The problem spiritually single wives have is that unless the Holy Spirit has revealed this command to our husbands, they get a free pass based purely on ignorance. We cannot play Holy Spirit and make demands of them to love us as Christ loved the church and still win them with our pure behavior. In fact, as soon as we begin to demand love as we define it or that is defined by something they don't know or believe in, we are no longer pure. We are the clanging cymbal in 1 Corinthians 13. Bong!

But there must have been some element of that love present in our early stages of love. How do we rekindle that? What are we willing to invest of our own selves to see that spark?

Our focus must be to create an atmosphere of peace and service in our home for the benefit of ourselves, our husbands, and our family. This brings glory to God. Then we must trust God to provide the love and transformation in our own lives from girlfriends if we don't get the support we need from our husbands.

Domestic Tranquility. Whatever domestic arrangements you made between the two of you, your husband expects you to abide by them and vice versa. In fact, you rely on each other to abide by them. Did you agree to stay home and manage the home and family while he works? Did you agree to work outside the home and help to provide income? Do you know he hates it when you squeeze the toothpaste tube in the middle, but you do it anyway? Does he love it when you retrieve the mail and deal with it? Does he like to have it laid out for his review? He loves it when you find joy in what you have built together and resist nagging him. He likes to feel like he is doing his part, you are doing your part, and everyone is happy.

My husband likes to think of me as his best friend. He knows I always have his best interest at heart. When we disagree most often it is because he will pardon someone who does not have his best interest at heart before I will. Long after he forgives people who harm him, I carry a grudge. My grudges cause us to argue until I eventually forgive too. As I have said before, Ed is more mature than me.

The arrangement we made before we married was that we would both work full-time and provide a good livelihood for our children. When we made our sixth move in eight years, this time as empty-nesters, the 10 years of information on my résumé included eight job changes, all related to my husband's relocations. We agreed my résumé looked like a game of hopscotch and I would stop working until he was in a location long enough for me to make an honest commitment to an employer. Since we made that agreement, I have served in various volunteer capacities and learned amazing things about what God is doing through charities in our new communities. Every time I start to look for a job instead of a volunteer opportunity, a new prospect pops up for my husband that requires a change in location. I consider that my answer from God about my career.

This has caused our domestic arrangement to change. My workload has increased dramatically on the home front. It has become understood that because I am home most days that I will handle all the domestic chores: laundry, cleaning, bill paying, financial planning, social directing, and travel plans. These are not really my strong suits, but our arrangement gives me the opportunity to serve God and become my husband's best friend every day. My husband is content with that and I am certain God likes it that way too since I experience such peace when I abide in this situation. But there is a part of me that is screaming "I am qualified to do more!" That part of me is writing this book. So through all the moves and changes, God has had a plan for my benefit all along.

> Her husband has full confidence in her and lacks nothing of value.
>
> She brings him good, not harm, all the days of her life.
>
> *Proverbs 31:11-12*

Our love and partnerships need to be lived out in real and honest ways. A husband needs to have full confidence in his wife and know that her service is dependable and genuine. By doing this, we are serving God and genuinely loving our husbands.

Physical Affection. So how much about this topic needs explanation? Your husband needs your love for him to culminate in physical affection — and that's spelled S-E-X. Especially after you have become a Christian, it is important to let your husband know that you have not become prudish. Think of Dana Carver's hyperbolic Church Lady from *Saturday Night Live*. This world has given Christian women a legacy of Puritanism. Since I dance on the fringe of the world, I have heard unbelievers' ideas that Christian women are tight-lipped and don't enjoy sex. Don't join the legend! This is never what God intended. It is important for your husband to experience the love of God through physical contact that is just as good as (or better!) than before you were a believer.[2] If there is a division between you and your husband that compromises mutual sexual pleasure, do all you can to restore it and find healing.

Pray for God's blessing on your marriage bed. One of the most real and vital ways to demonstrate the love of God is by sharing your body, the temple of the Holy Spirit. For many men, the best way they have to connect with you is physically. They just don't feel connected, generally, by talking like women do. I have been challenged by this thought, but I believe the physical love we share with our husbands is the closest thing an unsaved husband has to a spiritual experience.

For this reason a man will leave his father and mother and be united to his wife, and the two will become one flesh. This is a profound mystery but I am talking about Christ and the church...The wife must respect her husband.

Ephesians 5:31-32

The wife's body does not belong to her alone but also to her husband. In the same way, the husband's body does not belong to him alone but also to his wife. Do not deprive each other except by mutual consent and for a time, so that you may devote yourselves to prayer.

Then come together again so that Satan will not tempt you because of your lack of self-control. I say this as a concession, not as a command. I wish that all men were as I am. But each man has his own gift from God; one has this gift, another has that.

1 Corinthians 7:4-7

As the relationship between Christ and his church is complex and multi-faceted, so is ours with our husbands. Many men have unrealistic or even incompatible sexual desires that we cannot live up to. In Stormie Omartian's book, *The Power of a Praying Wife*,[3] she suggests that when you are not feeling up to the task, that you ask for twenty minutes to slip away and prepare. Take an "Esther moment!" Get out your slinky nightie and take a bath with candles and something that smells yummy, or jump into the shower, fluff up your hair, and do whatever it takes to feel pretty. During this time, turn your thoughts over to your desire for your husband. Ask God to help you — ask Him to be a part of this evening's romance.

I suggest for those of you who have frequent unwanted booty calls that you write this verse on a piece of paper, tuck it in a zip lock bag, and stick it to your shower or bath wall.

Don't just pretend that you love others. Really love them. Hate what is wrong. Stand on the side of the good. Love each other with genuine affection, and take delight in honoring each other. Never be lazy in your work, but serve the Lord enthusiastically. Be glad for all God is planning for you. Be patient in trouble, and always be prayerful.

Romans 12:9-12
New Living Translation

Now you are truly prepared to make love. I have had two experiences with this method. One outcome was that my husband had gone to sleep while I got prepared and the need had passed. Then the choice was mine: Should I wake him? The other experience I have had was amazing! It's a good thing I was prepared, because when I asked God to be a part of my sex life, the intensity increased and the experience was…well, spiritual! There was an extra dimension added to the sex that redefines union.

Taking Care of You

In order to best serve our husbands and our families we must first focus on our own personal walk with the Lord. When we abide in Him, we are better able to live up to the fullest potential God created in us. We are more open to the Holy Spirit's leadings in our day-to-day life, and since we are the primary godly influence in our home, it is imperative for us to remain strong. I encourage you to follow these three guidelines.

1) Examine your heart.

- Does your heart harbor feelings of resentment or bitterness towards your husband? If so, ask God to remove this bitterness from your heart. (This could also involve a closer look at where these feelings are coming from).

- Does your heart feel lonely? If so, ask God to fill you with His love, and to lead you to caring, understanding, and encouraging female friends.

- Does your heart hide doubtful feelings that your husband will ever be saved? If so, ask God to increase your faith.

The inventory above holds questions I have to ask myself routinely. Because I have moved so frequently, I am often in a position of being alone in a new place, having to make new friends without my husband. God is always faithful. He always leads me to people who are with me for the season that I live in a particular location and sometimes beyond the address change. I often say that I collect Christians. I have the assurance that if I move from their immediate community, we will labor together in our global community, and I will spend eternity in heaven with them. My husband sees a remarkable commitment level from the friends God has provided me. Their love and support is a monumental example of God's love that is available only in the Christian community.

2) Seek God everyday.

Try to find a private place in your home to quietly read your Bible and pray. This is a time for meditation and prayer, so it needs to be uninterrupted. Depending on how tolerant your husband is, you may not want to overtly read your Bible (or this book) in front of your husband, or make a point of telling him what you are doing.

When we moved to Michigan, I bought my own chair. I put it next to the fireplace and I sat there daily for morning conversations first with God and then with my husband. We have moved multiple times since then, but I still sit in that chair every morning for our first conversation of the day.

I am fortunate that my husband is supportive of my morning devotional time on most days. He knows that it refreshes me and he likes to see the optimistic, perky wife who is drawn out by my devotional time, rather than the multiple negative ways my personality can morph without an infusion of God's perspective.

Sometimes, just occasionally, my husband will come in at the tail end of my time with God, and it has been a way to use what I learned from the Bible and share something meaningful with him. It is really astounding how often what I read in the Bible correlates to what is going on in his life!

If your husband is not on board with your commitment, make your appointment with God when it is private and will not affect your husband. If a devotion time is not possible, learn to catch moments as you transition from one task to the next. For example, when you get the vacuum cleaner out and put it away. Or on your way to the grocery store or to pick up the kids from soccer practice. What would happen if you prayed every time you changed a diaper?

God is always there to listen when we speak, but if we want to hear God speak, most often, His voice comes in our quiet time.

3) Pray! Be specific in your prayers.

- Pray for yourself, for any struggles or issues you might be having in your marriage.

- Pray for God to protect your marriage from the enemy's grasp. Remember, Satan hates marriage, because it is a reflection of Christ's love for the Church. Instead, Satan loves to divide people, split marriages, and break homes. He would love to use our spiritually single situation against us. Imagine how thrilled Satan would be to use your church or your commitment to God to break up your marriage? That's a double win for the enemy.

- Pray for your husband (a good book to get is *The Power of a Praying Wife* by Stormie Omartian.)

- Pray for his salvation.

- Pray for God to guide him in his decisions (even if he isn't a believer).

- Pray for success in his job.

- Pray for Christian male friends to come into his life. Men are often more likely to follow the example of other men they admire, instead of following the example of their wives.

Rick Warren encourages us to "use 'breath prayers' throughout the day, as many Christians have done for centuries. You choose a brief sentence or a simple phrase that can be repeated to Jesus in one breath.' [4]

It may help you to keep a prayer journal so that you can keep track of what you pray and the answers you receive. I follow a prayer list that I adapted from the tables of contents of Stormie Omartian's *Power of Praying* books. I've applied the prayers to myself, my husband, and my children. Her books are structured with thirty chapters — a topic to pray for every day of the month.

Additionally, I have a list of five things I pray for weekly. I am on a couple of prayer chains that send e-mails daily. I jot lists for prayer just like I do my grocery list and tuck them into my Bible for the next morning. I try to keep an attitude of prayer all day long by visualizing Jesus in the next cubicle, the other chair, sitting shotgun when I drive, and directing the angels ahead of me to clear parking places that he hand selected for me (which does not always guarantee me a close parking space!). I am always amazed at the care and tenderness he shows me when I include him.

Examine your heart, seek God every day, and pray: These three steps are the same that are recommended to missionaries when they are sent on mission trips. Your home is your mission field. You can do these three things in the moments when your husband is not around and he will never know you did them. But I bet he will see the benefits!

Rick Warren's book, *The Purpose Driven Life,* makes a series of points that are very central for a healthy spiritually single life. He says we humans are hard-wired for five things in this order:

1. *Worship (to God)*

2. *Fellowship (with other believers)*

3. *Discipleship (accountability to a mentor and then becoming one ourselves)*

4. Ministry (to Christ's family)

5. Missions (to the world) [5]

Part of the reason we feel unstable is that we always skip ahead to missions and often we have not yet completed the first four steps adequately. How many times have you given up fellowship so you could be a good witness to your husband (your mission) and then had a miserable time, blown up, or resented him? Have you ever skipped a women's ministry or church event so that you could be with your husband, and then a friend who went told you how wonderful it was and you wished you had gone from the bottom of your toes? God built us for worship before missions, fellowship before missions, discipleship before missions, and ministry to Christ's family before missions. Though we have many more opportunities to be missionaries in our home than many others do, we have to balance it with healthy amounts of worship, fellowship, discipleship, and ministry during the times that won't affect our husbands. If not, we will find ourselves stressed, worn thin, and out of God's perfect order.

Two Dangerous Thoughts to Avoid

"If only I were a better wife (or better Christian), then my husband would be saved...."

"I must not be _____ (fill in the blank with the adjective of your choice) enough or else he'd be saved by now."

Shake these thoughts from your head and don't let them in again! At the very least, these are negative, unproductive thoughts. At worst, mistruths, half-truths, and full-blown lies can permeate your thoughts and do some serious damage. This is Satan trying to steal your joy by filling you with inadequacy. Remember: Only God can lead someone to salvation, and only that individual soul can choose to accept it or not. God knows your husband better than you do, and he knows the exact set of circumstances that may drive your husband to seek God. Are you brave enough to pray for those circumstances? Give your husband's salvation to God, and rest easy! God knows what's best for your husband and for you. He desires your husband's salvation even more than you do. Trust him for it.

The Next Wave

Piglet sidled up to Pooh from behind. 'Pooh,' he whispered.

'Yes, Piglet?'

'Nothing,' said Piglet, taking Pooh's paw, 'I just wanted to be sure of you.' [6]

Is your husband sure of you?

Six

Set Apart:
What Does Your Sanctification
Mean to Him?

What Is Sanctification?

Paul tells us in 1 Corinthians 7 that our husbands are "sanctified" through us because we are believers. What does sanctify mean? It means to purify or consecrate. Let's look at a couple of definitions for the word *sanctify*. First from Webster:

> **sanctify** *1 to set apart to a sacred purpose or to religious use : consecrate*
>
> *2 to free from sin : purify*
>
> *3 a to impart or impute sacredness, inviolability, or respect to b to give moral or social sanction to*
>
> *4 to make productive of holiness or piety <observe the day of the Sabbath, to sanctify it -- Deuteronomy 5:12[1]*

From *Baker's Evangelical Dictionary of Biblical Theology*, we learn that sanctify means: "...the state of proper functioning." In the theological sense, things are sanctified when they are used for the purpose God intends. A human being is sanctified, therefore, when he or she lives according to God's design and purpose. The Greek word translated as "sanctification" (hagiasmos) means "holiness." To sanctify, therefore, means "to make holy." The opposite of sanctified is "profane."

> *You must distinguish between the holy and the common, between the unclean and the clean,*
>
> *Leviticus 10:10* [2]

What is clean? What is unclean? If we are sanctified by living according to God's design and purpose, how does that translate to our partner? If we fail to live by God's design and purpose what then are the implications for our husbands? Our kids?

Your faith sanctifies you for God's purpose and makes you holy. Your faith sanctifies your husband and makes your husband holy. In the same article, *Baker's Evangelical Dictionary* goes on to say that one definition of *holy* is, "Belonging to, derived from, or associated with a divine power."[3] If your husband is like mine, the last thing on his mind is being holy. Don't misunderstand. He wants to be respected, but his idea of holy is Mother Theresa, Ghandi, or a rabbi. Though these are great people and great examples, he is not interested in sharing their identities. He's a regular guy with a lot on his mind. He just wants to know he doesn't have to worry about where his next pizza is coming from. But God's Spirit makes us holy, so whether or not our husbands fully comprehend it, the fact that we are children of God makes our husbands holy by default.

Baker's definition tells us the opposite of sanctified is common, unclean, or profane. Without you, that's what he becomes. In some instances, guys are just profane — no amount of female influence is going to have a visible effect on Larry the Cable Guy. If your man is like him, he may be a hoot to live with, but you may never see him civilized. That does not mean he is not sanctified, set apart to work God's intentions in your life, and to be influenced by you — or rather — God's Spirit in you. Between sanctified and profane, which legacy would you like your children to inherit from their father?

Your husband is set apart for a sacred purpose. There are probably various reasons he is in your life — you probably recited them in your wedding vows. He makes you laugh, he is a calming influence, he keeps you mentally strong, he knows just what you need, or as Tom Cruise says in *Jerry Maguire*, he "completes" you — but the most remarkable purpose your husband will serve, in my opinion, is as a tool to achieve God's sacred purpose in you!

Your husband's association with you puts him in a place of holiness, set apart for God's work, even if he doesn't realize his purpose. Although this does not bring him into a personal relationship with Jesus (that's a decision he has to make), your husband is, unwittingly, a resource God has blessed you with for your faith, personal growth, and development. He, too, is set apart to receive spiritual influence he would not otherwise have because of the presence of God's Spirit in you. God's Spirit will always draw people (believers and unbelievers) toward holiness and purity. Every blessing you receive as a child of God trickles over to your husband. Every judgment does, too. So, submission to God's authority and your husband's place in your home are paramount to the success of your mission.

Another reason to honor the sanctification connection with your husband is that your continued association with him makes your children clean and holy as well — otherwise, the children would likely be separated from the stability of your spiritual influence. We all want the best for our children on earth and in heaven, so it is really important to understand the order God created and the ways in which we as believers can live this out.

> *To the rest I say this (I, not the Lord): If any brother has a wife who is not a believer and she is willing to live with him, he must not divorce her. And if a woman has a husband who is not a believer and he is willing to live with her, she must not divorce him. For the unbelieving husband has been sanctified through his wife, and the unbelieving wife has been sanctified through her believing husband. Otherwise your children would be unclean, but as it is, they are holy. But if the unbeliever leaves, let him do so. A believing man or woman is not bound in such circumstances; God has called us to live in peace. How do you know, wife, whether you will save your husband? Or, how do you know, husband, whether you will save your wife?*
>
> *1 Corinthians 7:12-1 6*

We'll talk more specifically about the children in the next chapter. But the following story about my stepdaughters reveals how God used my spiritually single situation to draw me closer to Him.

Deeper With God

When I married my husband, we blended two families, and at times, not very successfully. His daughters lived with their mother out of state and we only got to see them on major school holidays. Every week, their dad called them to keep in touch, and occasionally he went to see them. Because I could not leave my kids to go see them, my relationship lacked even the limited continuity that their father had. Between visits, they had always grown up so much we hardly recognized them. As they approached their teen years, they decided not to come to our home for holidays because they had school activities and jobs. I objected, but my husband feared losing his own relationship with his daughters if he placed demands on them. We argued bitterly about that decision. It broke my heart because so much time lapsed between visits for me that I hardly knew them. It was not until my oldest stepdaughter's high school graduation invitation arrived addressed solely to my husband that we realized that the girls' decision not to visit us had eroded what little family structure we once shared. I was devastated. My husband was shocked. But that experience drove me to my knees in a whole new way. I needed God to fix what had gotten so messed up that it was impossible for a mere mortal stepmother to fix. I truly believe that I know God more personally today as a result of these circumstances. As my relationships have been renewed and repaired with my stepdaughters, I cherish every little experience with them. My understanding about God is dramatically changed because I had this experience along with my unbelieving husband. He has watched as I have submitted to God and he has seen my anger and hurt wax, wane, explode, and finally subside. He has watched as I have submitted to God's leading and learned to channel God's mercy and grace to young ladies who loved their dad, but did not know or care about me. Together we have marveled at the transformation in our family. We both consider it a miracle and true testament to what God can do in the life of a spiritually single wife through an unbelieving spouse.

Divorce

In C.S. Lewis' book The *Screwtape Letters,*[4] he shares with us his perspective on the communication between a subordinate spirit of darkness and his commanding officer as they strategize to trip up and destroy the faith of a new believer. I often think of my decisions and whether or not they bring joy to my Master or to my Master's enemy. I think weak relationships and divorce delight my Master's enemy and destroy some of the good we can do on earth. This is not my mission. I was divorced twenty years ago from a very nice Christian man who was struggling with maturity issues. I was not kind or very Christ-like when I gave up, abandoned our vows, and divorced him. I had maturity issues of my own. I know that the enemy got a foothold in my life and hardened my heart. It was easier to walk away from a struggling relationship than it was to stick with it and grow up. My rebellion gave me freedom from the struggle and a new start, but the cost was passed on to my children. Their stability, their future, their entire world has been affected negatively so I could be free. It was the most selfish decision I ever made with the most regrettable consequences.

One of the things I have taken with me from the divorce into my next marriage to a nonbeliever is to realize how sacred my vows are. It is important that we as spiritually single women realize that the enemy works in many ways to bring about the destruction of our marriages. How dare we, by our belief in Christ, bring sanctification to our husbands without salvation? By bringing sanctification to our husbands through Christ, we sanctify the entire next generation. I can imagine that causes a lot of contempt with our enemy and his henchmen.

If your marriage is in a rough spot, or you feel like distance is growing between you and your husband, it is important to bridge the gap. Reach out even if it is not your fault. If you don't feel love anymore and you would really like to lose the guy, ask God to show you how much God Himself loves your husband. Go back and watch The *Passion of the Christ*. Make yourself really watch the beatings Christ took. He took those lashes for the love He had for your husband. Give up on your husband? Maybe. But never give up on the love God has for him. Never give up on your mission to be the conduit for that love. Never underestimate what God can do in and through you and your children in your spiritually single situation.

How the Sacred May Affect Our Husbands

Let's get real here. Church is a subculture. Church people have their own language. They often call each other brother and sister and talk about "the blood." They sometimes sing songs with "thee" and "thou'" in the lyrics or about being "desperate" for God. They pray aloud using a lot flowery words and keep referring to God as "Father." If you grew up in church, you find comfort in the culture and acceptance there. If you strayed from it, you probably had a period of discomfort when you came back — trying to dodge the imaginary lightening bolts you would have sent to yourself if you were God.

But if a man has little or no church experience, and is married to a God-fearing woman — or worse, if he had a negative church experience — a new experience in the subculture of church with his wife probably induces more negative feelings than he cares to wrestle with. The loss of his partner on Sunday mornings, the guilt that comes from ignoring God, the repulsion of hearing about blood and redemption, or for those with partners of a different faith even the mention of Jesus' name can produce a knee jerk reaction to bolt. Remember this very important fact: Your husband's spiritual progress may not happen in church.

Recently, my husband and I went to a jazz concert. The snacks that were available at the concert were pretty gross and we were hungry when we left. My husband had recently met the owner of a small bar and grill in our neighborhood and wanted to go patronize his establishment. We decided to stop in for an appetizer, a drink, and a schmooze with the owner.

I walked in to the darkness and smelled the "old" smell: old smoke, old booze, old grease, old who-knows-what! I saw the place full of young, vibrant partyers singing karaoke country and western songs. I am not a fan of country and western music — remember, we had just left a jazz concert. They were having a blast and I felt old and dull. My husband was quite content, sipping his libation, and waiting for his onion rings. I, on the other hand, was visibly disturbed by my surroundings, not because they were bad or anything inappropriate was going on, but because I have baggage from growing up in a home with an alcoholic father.

When my husband went to the bathroom, an old drunk man staggered past my table (shades of my father) and said something unintelligible that I perceived as disgusting. It was like hearing a phonograph needle scratch an album — pure culture shock. I was repulsed. I could not wait to get out of there. I was experiencing the opposite of sacred — I was experiencing the profane.

I share that story because that same disturbed feeling is what my husband feels about my church. Just plain "Ick!" If our husbands ever come with us for a church service, we need to know where we will take them. It may not be to the church you go to regularly. I have found that "seeker churches" have been more helpful in bridging the gap between my non-believing husband's culture and my church culture.

More on the Profane

One of the imperative spiritual disciplines that helps us to grow is fellowship. Without it, our perspective becomes our own and we run the risk of missing out on other people's viewpoints and spiritual reflections. Left to our own devices, we can seriously misunderstand or misperceive what we are learning from God. It is also important to remember that as you share your situation with others, many people from church cultures would consider the line you walk between the sanctified and the profane difficult to understand and accept. Even the story above about going to a bar and grill could raise eyebrows in some church cultures. It's a fine line we all walk in learning to understand how to live "in" the world (i.e., not secluding ourselves in Christian subcultures) and yet not be "of" the world.

As a Christian woman married to a business executive, I often find myself in situations walking that line in the world. Just as Jesus called us to influence those who are lost, I have had the opportunity to host cocktail parties in my home for my husband's colleagues or go on extravagant dinners with executives and their wives. I have shopped for designer clothes in swanky boutiques and spent way more money than I ordinarily would so that I could float in the right circles to benefit my husband's career and have a spiritual presence in his world. I have had photo ops with local politicians, and I have had the influence to channel large sums of money to charities to build the communities we have lived in. I have gone on cruises and vacations in places that might be considered "racy" so that my husband could attend conferences or have a much-needed escape from the stress of his busy executive world. I have heard off-color stories, racist comments, and words of profanity. I have listened to the politically incorrect, the disingenuous, the lost, and the deceived. I have witnessed the excesses of people who don't even know they long for God. Would others judge me? Perhaps. But I thank God for every experience. The most brilliant opportunities I have had to share my Christian spirituality with others is while I am supporting my husband at what he does. If I was not submissive to and supportive of my husband, who would be there to speak God's love and life to the people in his world? I am where I am so that I can be available and effective in the missions God puts on my calendar.

If you find eyebrows raised in regard to your activities, take the issue to God. Humbly seek his guidance along with those whom you trust. This is when a mentor is so important. And when you are convinced about the activities in which you should be involved, go do them. Do them wholeheartedly for your husband and for the Lord as you bring honor to them both. Forgive anyone who might judge you and move on. Look for God's blessing in every opportunity. You may be called to the unchurched until God changes your situation. It may mean a change in church homes. It may mean having serious discussions within your fellowship group about what God has called you to do and how valuable it is even if it looks different from other ministries.

The Back-Slidden Husband

I want to switch gears as we wrap up our discussion on sanctification and take a look at those husbands who, at some point, really did make a personal decision for Christ — but something happened. They prayed the prayer, but now they are not walking their talk. Let's try to understand these partners. In her book, *Christianity is Jewish,* Edith Schaeffer discusses three aspects of salvation. She describes the first and third aspects as follows:

> ...First when a person understands what God has made clear and accepts the solution that God paid so dearly to make available, and accepts what has been accomplished on the cross...that person is immediately forgiven and cleansed from the guilt of all his or her sin...forever.

> The third thing ...is... that if they are in a plane crash, [or other such calamity]...and the soul is separated from the body, the teaching that 'to be

absent from the body is to be present with the Lord,' applies immediately. [5]

Mrs. Schaeffer goes on to say that what happens between the first and the third aspect of salvation is sanctification; a growth, a gradual change, but no person becomes perfect in this life until Jesus returns. Sanctification is a gradual process of perfecting our cleansing during our lifetime, so Christ can dwell in us. Our day-to-day life is a battle with the enemy. If your marriage is in this place, understand that Satan is your husband's enemy and Satan's "whole thrust is one of destruction, and what he tries to destroy in the 'born-again one' is peace, joy, longsuffering, gentleness, goodness, faith, meekness, temperance.... Satan, as he tries to attack, [causes] worm-eaten, blighted, wizened things to appear in the place of fruit." [6] The longer the separation from God goes on the more distorted the fruit becomes.

These guys are going to heaven! No matter how much grief they cause you, they once knew how it felt to be clean and guilt-free. Can you imagine how miserable these guys must feel to have known the forgiveness of God and be cleansed and guilt-free once, only to suffer (unwittingly?) under the destructive forces of Satan's attack? Could that explain some of the issues you deal with? Do you see a sense of the profane — the opposite of sanctified — at work in their lives?

Good News!

But there is good news. Your husband's association with you makes him pure and set aside for God's work, even if he doesn't realize his purpose. He is unwittingly a resource God has blessed you with for your support, personal growth, and development. Every blessing you receive as a child of God trickles over to your husband. Every judgment does too. So, submission to God's authority and your husband's place in your home is paramount to the success of your mission. In many instances, some of the consequences for your husband's unfaithfulness to God are passed over because God sees your faithfulness as a believer and you are one with your husband (I know, marriage is a mystery even Paul did not understand!)

So what does your sanctification mean to your husband? Only the entire legacy you will leave for all the generations to follow you. Will you leave a legacy of Christ's joy and fulfillment? I pray that's what your future family genealogists will find because of the history you are creating now.

The Next Wave

Did you know that your unbelieving husband has a privileged position in God's eyes? The apostle Paul told the believers in Corinth not to divorce an unbelieving spouse who is willing to stay, because that spouse is sanctified.

That word means several things. *Sanctified* means separation from evil things and ways. Another definition is "made holy." God is making us better every day. *Sanctified* as it pertains to unbelieving spouses and children, means "set apart." Because of the covenant relationship God makes with believers through Christ, he extends his blessing to include a "setting apart" of a believer's immediate family.

Every individual must make his or her own Christian commitment. This verse doesn't promise an instant, all-inclusive, family-pack salvation. It does, however, promise God's special attention. As the Lord blesses me, his child, the blessing spills over onto my husband.[7]

Seven

What About My Children?

If He Doesn't Believe, Is There Hope for My Children?

For most of us, when we got married to our unbelieving husbands, the last thing on our radar screen was a relationship with God. Oftentimes when you experience the miracle of birth, God blips onto the radar screen for the first time. As mothers we begin to see the importance of faith in a creator. We know that growing a healthy baby doesn't just happen in our tummies. We know that God had something to do with it. As our faith grows, we know innately that it is important, perhaps imperative, to share that faith with our children. As we begin our own journey and a relationship with God develops, we learn how important it is for our children to know God and see God in us. But what if Dad doesn't understand it? Our children — each one a walking, talking, breathing miracle — remind us of ourselves, our husband, and our God. We realize that we did not create a child so perfect alone. The love we experience with and for our children is like nothing else we have ever experienced.

We want to raise our children well and be good moms on every level. Physically, we want to provide for their every need; emotionally, we want to help them feel loved, become stable, secure, and independent; spiritually, uh-oh, what do we want? Do we want our kids to know God? How do we teach them? Where does their dad fit into this aspect of their growth?

The End Game

In Lee and Leslie Strobel's book, *Surviving a Spiritual Mismatch*, they remark that one thing that nearly all parents can agree upon is that we want our children to grow up with a strong moral compass that prevents them from making bad choices as they grow older and get into negative peer-pressure situations. We want them to feel good about themselves, have the courage to become leaders, and earn our trust as well as the trust of other children and parents. Where will they learn these things? Who can we engage to help us to teach them?

Do we want our children to grow up loving and fearing God, as well as loving and respecting both parents? Do we want them to know Jesus offers them salvation? Do we want them to feel confident in themselves? Do we want them to recognize their blessings and be kind to family members and others in their circle? If you answered yes to any of these questions, then you want to raise followers of Christ. You want them to be happy, productive, believe in Jesus, and to become Christ-like. You may realize now that you are the only example of Christ your children ever see modeled in their formative years. That's profound.

Values

If values are caught, not taught, what are you as a believer and your husband as a nonbeliever, teaching your children? [1] If you experience friction with your husband, or if your husband openly disagrees with you about your children's spiritual development, there are other strategic approaches to take. The most important lesson for you is to have these discussions with your husband privately outside the earshot of your children. If there is any disagreement with their spiritual training, it must be handled between you so that you can present a loving, united front. It might be helpful to remember that Jesus is the prize, not the battlefield.

Even the smallest of children sense when there is tension in the home. As the children grow older, they sense the difference in value systems between their parents. Dad may be more open to missing church for a football game or taking the kids to an R-rated movie that Mom might forbid. If you take your children to church and Dad does not come, Dad's disinterest can be an example for our children to learn rebellion. How do we deal with that? Sometimes, in an effort to combat Dad's disinterest, we will over-react and become rigid, representing God as harsh and inflexible. "No, Johnny, you may not go to the game on Sunday morning with Dad, that's the Lord's Day." Is this the God we think our children will learn to love? Dad has a ministry with his children too, and it may happen on Sundays sometimes. Can we stand back and bless it in Jesus' name?

Sometimes an apathetic or indecisive Dad will suggest that "we raise the children till they are old enough to choose their own spiritual path." That sounds very enlightened and sophisticated, but what we create is a spiritual vacuum in our homes. There is no God.

What happens in a culture without God? According to Joseph Campbell, our longing for a god causes us to create our own gods.[2] Every religion has a hero or a prophet who saves man by his connection with the Divine. There is Mohammed, Buddha, Moses, and Jesus.

An example in Exodus tells us that even after God led the children of Israel out of captivity under the most miraculous circumstances ever recorded in human history, the Israelites created their own god. In Moses' absence, while he met God on Mount Sinai for

40 days, the Israelites experienced such a spiritual vacuum that they created a golden calf to worship. That turnaround only took six weeks! What makes us think our children would be any less susceptible to human nature?

Our culture (full of the false gods of this world) is ready to lure our children into many profound ideologies (from materialism to hedonism to intellectualism, or how about "techno-ism?") that will lead them away from the moral codes even our non-believing husbands want for their children.

> *Jesus said, "Let the little children come to me, and do not hinder them, for the kingdom of heaven belongs to such as these."*
>
> *Matthew 19:14*

So our best approach is to provide a spiritual education. Approach it as you would choosing a school. Interact with different programs at different churches until you find one that fits your family values well.

Lee and Leslie Strobel tell us in *Surviving a Spiritual Mismatch* that frequently, non-believing parents allow their children to go to Sunday school. A recent study shows that 48% of non-churched parents send their kids to Sunday school. The reason? Many believe that the moral training that they received in public schools during their youth is no longer available for their kids. If the church can help, many parents are all for it.

If your spouse is worried about what his children are being taught at Sunday school, encourage him to personally check out the curriculum as if it were a private school. Most of the stories revolve around God's love and have important morals and values that we all want to instill in our children.[3]

Ground Rules

As you and your husband make decisions regarding your children, there are certain ground rules that all households need to have, but especially so in a home where there is a spiritually single situation.

First, all questions are permissible and all feelings are legitimate.[4] Children have lots of questions and as parents we need to have straight answers that support open, honest discussions. You and your spouse need to have answers ready for questions like, "If church is so important, why isn't Daddy going?" "Are you mad at Daddy?" This one is usually in response to watching their mother stomp through the house and slam cupboard doors on their way out the door on Sunday morning. When children sense tension, it can trigger fear and uncertainty. Validate their feelings. "Mom and Dad have a difference of opinion, just like you and Sara did over the new puppy today. But just like you and Sara are still best friends, Dad and I are still best friends too." Always give them the reassurance that you and their dad are in a permanent relationship and so are they.

Avoid turning your kids against your spouse.[5] As we begin to build in our children some basic biblical values, we send the message that it is wonderful to know Jesus in a personal way, to pray, and to go to church. So conversely, if Dad doesn't know Jesus in a personal way, and pray, and go to church, will the children begin to reason that there is something inferior about him? It will be our job to set an example of loving acceptance. Depending on the age of the children, they can be told that everyone has a choice about loving Jesus and how each person shows love to Jesus. Daddy has made a choice that is different from ours, but Jesus loves Daddy too. "Why do I have to go to church if Dad doesn't?" Our answer must be that it is very important to learn about Jesus now so that when they are adults like Mommy and Daddy, they will make good choices too.

There will be many times when the care and preparation of your children on Sunday mornings as a one-woman job is overwhelming and exhausting. The sheer frustration may cause you to snap while your husband sleeps in or relaxes with a second cup of coffee. How you handle these moments verbally and non-verbally will be some of the most profound lessons you teach your family. Remember our 1 Peter 3 model: We want our husband and family to be won without words. Is Mommy mad? Is Mommy expecting too much? Perfect appearance on Sunday morning is not the goal. Being punctual is nice, but it is not the end of the world if you arrive late. Start preparing the night before and avoid the last minute tension. Don't beat yourself up or your kids. The road to church on Sunday mornings is filled with potholes that can absolutely derail you, your efforts to be Christ-like, and your children's spiritual growth.

In an episode of *Everybody Loves Raymond*, his family is leaving for church while he stays behind. When his children ask why Daddy isn't going to church, his wife Deborah encourages them to ask their Dad. She never answers for him. Later, in private, Deborah and Ray have a hilarious discussion about hypocrisy, his own guilt overwhelms him, and he commits to attend church regularly. This example, although not based on reality, demonstrates something very important for us as spiritually single women. Be very careful to carry your respect and honor for your husband into the parenting arena for your children to see. Make sure your discussions with your husband about spiritual things are private. Allow God the time to mold your husband to become the man he was designed to be.

Never criticize your husband in front of the children. One of the lessons we learned from Raymond's wife is to address things privately with your husband. Whether it is the children's spiritual training or the budget, make a time without children present to discuss the direction you would like to go. Ask him to grant you the same favor of not criticizing you in front of the children as well. This is not only good for both of you, but it provides security for your children. A united front is always a firm foundation for your children.

Give your husband a heads up when possible. When you know your kids are going to have a spiritual milestone, try to give your husband a heads up so that he can be prepared with an appropriate response. Perhaps they are making a decision about salvation, baptism, a mission trip or even church camp. If you can brief your husband and let him know that you consider this a significant spiritual milestone, it will prepare him to bless them.

My friend Judy is married to a great guy who is Jewish. They have two young teens who have been raised in a Christian community all their lives. There have never been any secrets about the direction her children have chosen, but perhaps he did not notice it like Judy did. The children went to summer camp through their church and Judy, suspecting that her children would have a "mountain-top experience," prepared her husband for their homecoming. She was so wise! Her children came home praising God and without Judy's preparation their dad, who had never before had such a transformational experience, would not have known how to react.

Sharing the Mission

> *Even a child is known by his actions, by whether his conduct is pure and right.*
>
> *Proverbs 20:11*

As our children become believers, they too will discover God's heart for your husband and their dad. Children can sometimes say things when it is not appropriate for us as wives to say them. I remember my niece, when she was growing up, went away to church camp and came home on fire for God. She accepted Christ at age ten and it did not take long for her to realize her mom loved God, but Dad was a little indifferent. As she grew older and into a young woman, she became more concerned about her dad's relationship with God. Her unwavering love and concern for her dad — even through some grumpy years — has ushered her dad into a relationship with God that is relevant and real. What a blessing it has been for her mom to have her daughter sharing the mission within their own family.

As your children grow in the Lord, they may become laborers in the field with you. As tiny children, asking Dad to routinely say bedtime prayers maybe the first step in his spiritual journey as well as your children's. If you make prayer the last step of the nighttime routine, it can be very soothing for a child going to sleep. Depending on their age, you as parents can decide on a prayer to recite each night, pray "free-style," or a combination of both. Children who feel free to ask questions can use this time to ask Dad about God and ask questions about blessings. It can drive Dad into a deeper relationship with his children and his God.

The Big Question

Many faiths do not promise an afterlife, but Christianity does. As your children mature, they will begin to notice the difference in your commitment level when compared to their dad. The big question will come when they grasp eternal life: Is my Daddy going to heaven? What will your answer be to that? How will your husband answer? An answer, which can be modified according to their age and understanding, is to tell them that God works his way into each person's heart a little differently and at a different pace. We need to pray and set a good example of who Jesus is as well as we can so that Daddy wants to love Jesus and go to heaven too.

The Next Wave

As my two daughters grew up, I often wondered what they thought about marriage. From being raised in church, they knew that God's ideal is one man, one woman, and their children all in agreement in matters of faith. But in our family, their dad didn't share our faith.

As the mom, my feelings and thoughts ran the gamut. I worried that somehow I was setting a bad example because I wasn't providing my children with God's best. I feared that they would marry unbelievers themselves, since that's what they were used to in our family. Even though my husband and I were both unbelievers when we got married, I still felt guilty.

Eventually, I came to accept that I could only do my best to be an example of a Christian wife and trust that God would fill in the gaps. Still, sometimes I wondered about what kind of an example I was setting for my girls.

Just before my oldest daughter got married (to a Christian man), I asked her what she had learned about marriage from watching her dad and me. After some thought she said, "I've learned that it's not always easy and that when things get tough, not to give up or give in because tough times don't last forever."

It is possible to impact my children positively for God's kingdom.

Nancy Kennedy [6]

Eight

Rapport: Finding Common Ground

Respect what is right in the sight of all men. If possible, so far as it depends on you, be at peace with all men.

ROMANS 12:17-18

Is It Rapport or Is It Secular?

In Christian homes, rapport is built on common beliefs between parents that are inculcated in their children. But what happens in a spiritually single home? If Dad's beliefs, or lack of belief, are different from Mom's how do we bridge the gap? What beliefs will be inculcated in the children of these marriages? I am going to suggest something that I would not suggest in a Christian home. I suggest that secularism may be a stepping-stone to bridge the gap. It takes the power of God out of the interaction, but it keeps the interaction flowing. Please hear me out.

There are many meanings for the word *secular*, but for the purpose of discussion in this chapter, we will use a definition from the *Oxford Concise Dictionary of the Christian Church*. Secularism refers to "a system which seeks to order and interpret life based on principles taken solely from this world, without recourse to a belief in God and a future life." [1] Though there have been many definitions since the word was coined in 1850, most of them are inconsistent with the church and bordering on heresy. I don't think that is the world we live in today. I think the lines have blended and many biblical principles have made their way into many secular ideologies. I was struck after September 11, 2001 when our country decided to use the phrase "Never forget!" How close it sounds to the instructions God gave the Israelites regarding their battle with the Amalekites in Deuteronomy 25:19: "Do not forget!"

If you look at the guiding principles in many of the books written by the most apparently secular authors, such as Anthony Robbins or even Marianne Williamson, you can identify many biblical principles. A common quote on the Internet by Marianne Williamson says: "And as we let our own light shine, we unconsciously give other people permission to do the same. As we are liberated from our fear, our presence automatically liberates others." [2] Matthew 5:14-16 says it better and his words have been around for nearly 2,000 years.

> *You are the light of the world. A city on a hill cannot be hidden. Neither do people light a lamp and put it under a bowl. Instead they put it on its stand, and it gives light to everyone in the house. In the same way, let your light shine before men, that they may see your good deeds and praise your Father in heaven." Why do secular teachings work? Because they spring from the truth of God and His truth sets us free.*

Secularism is a way for us to order and interpret our own lives by principles that bring us whatever we call success. Every social system must have some agreed standards and to that end we have local, state, and federal laws that govern our behavior. In a secular society, our principles must include those standards, and we must create our lifestyle within the restraints of our social system or risk individual failure, social ostracism, and/or going to jail. Within that system, as people find their own success based on their own principles, there is no guilt, no sin, and no failure as long as they don't get caught breaking the law.

The condition most of our husbands function within and understand best is somewhere on the continuum of secularism. By association, we as their spiritually single wives live in a secular environment every day. Volumes have been written on how secular humanism erodes Christian values, but I think understanding a secular orientation is a common ground that helps us build valuable rapport with the unsaved who need a transformation most — especially our husbands.

While we were unbelievers, we were also somewhere on a secular journey that would have lead to eventual destruction, death, and separation from God. If you can remember your own days before Christ, you know the bigger problem was that until Jesus rescued you from your own secular path, you didn't even know where you were headed.

God is not relevant in secularism. It is possible to spend an entire lifetime and never know God or realize that we ever caught a glimpse of Him. Thank God that He sent someone who would look past my secular striving for perfection and love me for who Jesus created me to be. That was the beginning of my transformation for which I am eternally grateful (quite literally). My prayer is that

God sends someone who loves Ed the way Jesus does so his transformation begins too.

If your unbelieving husband lives according to a secular interpretation of our world, how do you reach him? I believe that we must start to build rapport by embracing the principles and order that your husband has adopted.

Choose Your Battles

In my husband's secular world, one of the principles he lives by is "loving relationships include sex." Surprise. I am sure that your husband has the same great idea. Our physical relationship is a wonderful way to build rapport in a way that my husband truly understands. It works well for us in marriage, but as our kids have grown older and developed loving relationships with the people they would later marry, do we still embrace that "loving relationships include sex"… before marriage?

In my husband's value system, he could embrace his children living with their partners and coming home with them to share a bed in our guest room. In my Christian world, until they were married, they could sleep in twin beds or separate rooms. But I knew I would have to reframe that argument in order to satisfy both his and my value systems. I made my argument based on a secular principle. I am an illegitimate child. As a result of my experience, I have grown to adulthood with many misconceptions about dads and family life that took me years to unlearn. My husband has been with me through some of those struggles. Our children may all make their own choices as adults in their world, but I would prefer our home and our world not be used — even for a weekend — to perpetuate a future generation that might struggle with similar misconceptions. In most instances, I was respected. Would I have been respected if I had quoted the seventh of the Ten Commandments? Picture it: Any spiritually single wife standing with arms raised up barking from Deuteronomy 5:18, "You shall not commit adultery." Even if thunderbolts and lightening accompanied it, I am certain that it would be a losing argument in a secular environment.

Building Rapport

If we embrace our husbands' value system, it puts us in a unique situation to share experiences and build rapport with our husbands in a way no one else can. If his value system focuses on the accumulation of wealth or the collection of goods and experiences, find the best way you can to support him. If it is about his career aspirations, look for ways that will allow him to succeed. If he loves his family more than anything else, allow him the opportunity to focus on that. Talk Dad up to his kids. Even if you know he is chasing after wind, you cannot tell him that — that is the job of the Holy Spirit.

My husband is really ambitious about his career. He also loves his children, and this often conflicted with his career. When we moved so that he could climb the career ladder he loved, our children — once they reached adulthood — often stayed behind to maintain their in-state college tuition. We did not want to leave our children, but Ed could not achieve his career objectives by staying in the same job.

The best way for me to support him was to keep his personal life in order — stay in touch with family members, make vacation plans for visits with our kids, plan graduation parties and weddings, manage the home maintenance schedule, budget and plan our finances, pay the bills, and be available to accompany him when his job required him to travel. In 2004, we modified our domestic arrangement when we moved to Michigan and I have not gone back to being employed full time. I stopped working in my career to be his full-time support.

Never in a million years would I have supposed that I would become the Helpy Helperton that I have become. Frankly, my family will attest that it would be more likely for me to expect the man in my life to serve me! But the most amazing thing happened when I adjusted to my husband's value system. As I embraced his career, supported his need to change geographic locations multiple times, and reverently took on the fallout from those career decisions in our personal life, God gave me time to pursue what I love — God's values. I got the privilege of serving God in various charities and church activities during the day while my husband was occupied with what he valued most in his career. I learned to work heartily as unto the Lord for my husband and serve God by serving Ed. I became less focused on myself and more focused on what God is doing in my husband and the communities in which his career has led us. It gave me time to write this book. It has been a great gig.

So just as we learned that we have the ability through our salvation and sanctification to sanctify our unsaved husbands for the work God intended for them, we as spiritually single wives have the ability to build rapport. We can influence the secular society our husbands have created in our home, because of our transformation by the power of the Holy Spirit. As we grow and learn spiritual principles, many times we will find compatibility with some secular principles our husbands practice.

The Wife of Noble Character

I find encouragement and direction every time I read Proverbs 31 though I must confess that as a new Christian, I laughed when I read it because it seemed so unattainable. The passage is written to a culture that was far more agrarian than the one in which most of us live, but with a little adaptation we can apply it to our own. If we use the text as God's blueprint for a wife and integrate it with our husband's value system we have a valuable equation for rapport.

A wife of noble character who can find? She is worth far more than rubies. I believe your self-worth is the framework — the very measurements of what the blueprint will ultimately build. Did your husband find a wife with a solid character? Is she worth far more than rubies? Do you value yourself that much? Above rubies? When we value ourselves that much, it empowers us to look eye-to-eye with others and speak truth with love. When I value myself it gives me freedom from intimidation and judgment.

Her husband has full confidence in her and lacks nothing of value. She brings him good, not harm, all the days of her life. The confidence we build with our husbands is the support structure of the blueprint. Without strong support, our structure erodes, but with strong support, it will last a lifetime. In most structures, we may not even realize that supports are integrated, but without them, the structure wouldn't stand.

She selects wool and flax and works with eager hands. A blueprint indicates the types of materials and the types of professionals needed to accomplish the construction of the structure. As wives, it is our job to choose products and be industrious in our homes.

She is like the merchant ships, bringing her food from afar. Often the blueprint will identify a particular type of material or fixture that may not be readily available, but will enhance the structure if we seek quality from other sources. Are you a shopper? Are you thrifty?

She gets up while it is still dark; she provides food for her family and portions for her servant girls. Every blueprint requires time management. Some days the blueprint has to allow for early starts in order to get every step in a certain process done. If you feed the workers on the work site, it keeps everyone on task.

She considers a field and buys it; out of her earnings she plants a vineyard. The business-savvy woman knows that a blueprint without a budget is never more than a dream. If you want the plan to have tangible results, you have to commit dollars to it and make sacrifices.

She sets about her work vigorously; her arms are strong for her tasks. She sees that her trading is profitable, and her lamp does not go out at night. In her hand she holds the distaff and grasps the spindle with her fingers. The woman who takes care of herself can commit to long hours and hard work because like any professional, she is equipped for her tasks.

She opens her arms to the poor and extends her hands to the needy. No matter how busy we get with a plan, or how involved the blueprint becomes, the women God designed us to be are still charitable. This one virtue should set us apart from all others.

When it snows, she has no fear for her household; for all of them are clothed in scarlet. Blueprints always take into account the types of weather the structure will have to withstand. A roof in Arizona will be different from a roof in Michigan because the weather conditions are entirely different. The blueprint helps us make decisions that are practical.

She makes coverings for her bed; she is clothed in fine linen and purple. In this blueprint, the fabrics chosen for the most intimate space in the structure — as well as the woman who created them — are fashionable, fine, and lovely. It is really important for our husbands and ourselves that we project an image of a woman satisfied and well cared for.

Her husband is respected at the city gate, where he takes his seat among the elders of the land. Once the structure is built, it is a direct reflection of the designer and its occupants. The public image of our husband is a direct reflection of how we demonstrate our respectful support. I believe this passage is the precursor to the adage that "behind every successful man is a supportive wife."

She makes linen garments and sells them, and supplies the merchants with sashes. In this plan, once the structure is underway, it is really important for us to be resourceful and find creative ways to generate income that are appropriate with our family situation. Whether you work a full-time job, a part-time job, have a home-based business, or don't work at all, you have resources that God's kingdom needs: time, clothes that need to be donated, or a service or meal that you can provide for someone in need. To undergird your success, you must use your resources wisely.

She is clothed with strength and dignity; she can laugh at the days to come. This woman is prepared for the future to such a degree that she exudes strength and dignity. Do we dare laugh at the future?

She speaks with wisdom, and faithful instruction is on her tongue. When this woman speaks, she demonstrates that she is both smart and wise. She has learned from both experience and from godly counsel, and she graciously passes that along to others.

She watches over the affairs of her household and does not eat the bread of idleness. Even after this woman of our blueprint has finished the plan, made her dreams a reality, and laughs at the future, she remains active so that the affairs of her household are purposefully planned.

Her children arise and call her blessed; her husband also, and he praises her: "Many women do noble things, but you surpass them all." This is the best part of the blueprint for any woman, but especially the spiritually single. When your actions speak loudly enough that you are respected by family, you can see and feel your own success.

Charm is deceptive, and beauty is fleeting; but a woman who fears the Lord is to be praised. Give her the reward she has earned, and let her works bring her praise at the city gate. Nothing is as empty as a person striving to achieve a goal for the recognition of others; however, when a woman is respected by others as a reflection of the good she has done, the blueprint has yielded the structure that God intended in her.

By applying Proverbs 31 to our own lives, we discover seventeen important traits that God intended for spiritually single wives to be and/or to have:

- self-worth
- confidence of her husband
- industry
- seeks quality
- time management
- business-savvy
- equipped for the tasks she takes on
- charitable
- practical
- fashionable
- respectful
- resourceful
- prepared for the future
- smart and wise
- active
- respected by family
- respected by others

So if you are *not* totally overwhelmed by all that this "Proverbs 31 Woman" does, please put this book down. My words cannot help you. But if — like me — you are overwhelmed, please take a breath and relax. This is a blueprint. No one expects us to be the finished project today. It will take us a lifetime to accomplish, but if we use the above list and align it with the values of our husbands, we now have the blueprint to build a better rapport with our husbands. Choose just one or two traits and aspire to them in ways that he will value. The more we aspire to the many traits that she possesses, the more blessed our husbands become. Do they call it blessing in their secular world? No. They call it success.

The Next Wave

When I am talking to somebody there are always two conversations going on. The first is on the surface, the other is beneath the surface on the level of the heart — and my heart is either communicating that I like the person I am talking to or I don't. God wants both conversations to be true. That is, we are supposed to speak the truth in love. If both conversations are not true, God is not involved in the exchange. We are on our own and on our own we will lead people astray. The Bible says that if you talk to somebody with your mouth and your heart does not love them, you are like a person standing there smashing two cymbals together. You are only annoying everybody around you. I ask God to make it so both conversations, the one from the mouth and the one from the heart, are true.[3]

Nine

Keep It Real

If I speak in the tongues of men and of angels,

but have not love, I am only a resounding gong

or a clanging cymbal.

1 CORINTHIANS 13:1

Are You Still Magically in Love with Your Husband?

There is no way to fake love, at least not for long. I can't imagine which would be worse: to pretend I love someone or to find out someone has been pretending to love me. But here is the premise with which we must love: Love is a decision, not a feeling. When we make the decision to love, magical things happen! Maybe not overnight, but feelings will never sustain our connection. The role we have in the life of our husbands has been, is now, and always will be to love them no matter what. It's a decision, an agreement, a vow every day that we must renew by our actions. That is how we keep it real.

In Gary Chapman's book, *The Five Love Languages*, he outlines five ways that we might "speak love" [1] to our husbands and sense love from him. If you have not already read *The Five Love Languages*, I highly recommend it. Unless we speak love in the language our husband understands, we might as well be speaking a foreign language. Those five different love languages are:

1. Words of Affirmation
2. Quality Time
3. Receiving Gifts
4. Acts of Service
5. Physical Touch

Lucky for my husband, I am conversant in all five languages, so it is very easy to shower me with love. But in order for me to shower my husband with love, I have to speak the languages that speak to him the best. Because my husband is a busy executive, it is really important for me to perform acts of service: the laundry, the dry cleaning, the errand running, and the social calendar. What I do during the week may never be noticed — unless I forget something and it has to be done on the weekend. If I chose not to do those mid-week tasks and instead gave my husband a gift, I would not be living and loving my husband authentically. It would be meaningless. My husband does not speak "receiving gifts" as a love language. Our history indicates he is very uncomfortable with receiving gifts. Even though I love to give gifts, I know that love language will not have an impact on him.

I am sure that as you look at Chapman's love languages that you can pinpoint the ones that your husband speaks best. Or just ask him! Use that information to your advantage and learn to really love your husband authentically. If you can fan the flame of your love, it increases your opportunity to love him the way God loves him.

Using Love to Make God Personal

My friend Lori began attending church while her children were young. Her husband, Steve, was invited by a client almost as a "business thing." Lori and Steve began a process of attending a church service each Sunday and tried a few different churches. Lori began to change and Steve became a little leery of the transformation that he saw in his wife. He liked the old Lori just fine. An influential client invited Steve to a Bible study during their lunch hour. Steve attended partly because of who it was that invited him and also because he felt like it would be a good way to understand what his wife was doing, learning about, and dealing with. At the Bible study, the Old Testament story of Moses and the burning bush was used as an example and the Holy Spirit triggered an epiphany for Steve. He came home to Lori with his new revelation: "You are like the burning bush! The bush was there and Moses could recognize it and see it through the fire, but he wasn't afraid. He knew it was God. You are just the same as the burning bush. You are still my Lori. I see you and recognize you, you're just on fire!" Just like Moses was not afraid, Steve was not afraid anymore either.

Lori's love for Steve had remained authentic as she began to fall in love with her Savior. She had continued to love Steve, but now she was burning with love for him and everyone else — just like God burns with love for each of us, including our unsaved husbands. We need to be God's hands and feet on the ground here on earth. We need to reach out to our mates and love them using the language that they speak. Our love needs to burn like Moses' burning bush.

Focus on Love to Avoid Sabotaging the Relationship

Once we have firmly established or re-established a loving relationship with our husbands, it is really important to avoid some of the most human things that sabotage our purpose. First of all, we have to know, love, and embrace freedom. He who the Son sets free is free indeed (John 8:36). As "free" wives, we must remember that we have escaped judgment. We can no longer use judgment, self-righteousness, and bondage to measure others, especially our unsaved husbands. We must use our freedom to demonstrate the love of God in us.

Matthew 7:1 says, "Do not judge, or you too will be judged." That is a Christian principle that should not be taken lightly. I struggle with this because we live in a society that makes rules and judgments based on looks, behavior, resources, gender, and any number of factors. So, if I judge someone because "they don't come to my church" (or just fill in the quotes with your pet peeve), am I saying they are not worthy of my company? Or that I am too highfalutin to be near them? God's principles will stand the test of time and eternity, but rules that separate people create obstacles that cause non-Christians to suffer. I even question the value of such judgments amongst believers. Anytime I can be better than the next sinner based on my behavior, the system is as flawed as I am. The extension of grace is so much more effective for transformation. Let's keep it real. It's so much more like Jesus would have lived.

Barriers to Keeping It Real

Hypocrisy. Ever gotten a whiff of food spoiling in the fridge? Stinky! So it is with hypocrisy. Our husbands may be very sensitive to inconsistencies and sniff out hypocrisy before the wind gets a chance to shift direction. It takes a long time to plant the ideas in our husbands' thoughts that being a Christian does not make us perfect; it is only a decision to aspire to follow Christ's example as best we can.

I live in my home trying my best to set the example of Christ on a minute-by-minute basis. I never know when or if my husband catches me doing something right; but I keep working diligently doing what God has called me to do. What sets me back? When my husband is affected by one hypocritical move by me, or any other Christian, and that causes him to question all the examples I have set, all the ideas I have suggested. My husband comes home dismayed or angry because he expected more from a professing Christian. I model forgiveness for my husband.

In these instances, I assure my husband that there will be many hypocrites in hell, but there will be a good number of us in heaven too! I have learned to make the argument that hypocrites are at the office, in the supermarket, at the bank, in the bars and back alleys, as well as in churches. If I can show God's love and forgiveness to my husband during his angry tirade about hypocrisy and then extend it to the hypocrite, I have demonstrated God's love in a very tangible way.

Self-righteousness. Nothing reduces a relationship to fragility faster than when one person considers himself or herself more righteous than the other. One of the key things I had to realize about my relationship with my husband is that the slightest hint of not accepting his faith was destructive. My husband often says his "religion is personal," meaning that he does not express it in a public way. He does not talk about faith or religion much. He does not pray openly, but is usually amenable to praying with me when I ask. He occasionally mentions God in his life, usually in the context of the many blessings which make him grateful. The truth is, God is not on his radar screen.

As a self-professed evangelical Christian, my relationship with God is personal, but my lifestyle is supposed to shine enough to make others interested in what makes me different. To share my faith openly and compare it to his would be seen as self-righteousness. It has been a personal exercise in discipline to keep my mouth shut and let my light shine. But that is what love, and God, require of me in this environment. That's how I keep it real.

Legalism. There are a lot of principles I try to follow: daily devotionals and prayer time, church attendance, worship through giving, service, and fellowship. I do those things for my own benefit as a person and as a Christian. There are blessings associated with all those things and I love being the beneficiary of those blessings. I am fortunate to live in a country and circumstances where I can choose to do those things. Each of those principles can become entrenched in us and bear great fruit. But in a spiritually single situation, that entrenchment can become legalism and derail the loving relationship that we are trying to nurture with our unsaved husbands. Webster tells us that legalism is "strict, literal, or excessive conformity to the law or to a religious or moral code." [2]

When we approach the topic of legalism, the first issue that always comes up in spiritually single situations is tithing. Someone might ask, "How can a spiritually single woman tithe, when her husband doesn't share her beliefs?" This is a great place to share your beliefs in a really personal and powerful way.

If you read the Old Testament, giving was more like taxation. The Israelites were required to sacrifice the best of their animals, wine, flour, and oil. These sacrifices occurred daily, weekly, monthly, and at festivals. So, it appears that if we use scripture as a reference point, giving a compulsory 10 percent would just be the beginning. We would have to give so much more to truly tithe, according to scripture, that it could become a major stumbling block in a relationship in which both partners did not agree. If I got legalistic and pressed my husband with the ten-percent law, I would lose him. All in favor of abandoning that idea, read on!

Our men are the hunter-gatherers of our species and I have never met a man who was not really serious about money management. The Christians did not invent debt-free living, but we have more resources in the Christian community than anywhere else on this topic. My husband has read and embraced the teachings in *The Total Money Makeover* by Dave Ramsey. Many of the arguments my husband and I have had about money have been settled through the biblical principles that Ramsey teaches (Ed was right, I was wrong, go figure). Ramsey teaches that we should give 10 percent, save 10 percent, and live on 80 percent. We should pay cash as we go and save for large purchases rather than incur debt. It has been one of the most powerful evangelical tools I have ever used in my home. It has really made a difference in how we look at our money and use it. There have been some painful, personal adjustments and sacrifices I have had to make to become debt-free. My perfect set of false nails has been gone for years, and I have to keep impeccable records in minute detail — no fudging. It takes a lot of time. But the upside is that I have the trust and honor of my husband. And after a while, my own nails have kind of grown on me.[3]

But the real question is still unanswered: What about tithing? I have an agreement with my husband and a separate agreement with God. My agreement with my husband goes like this: He gets to give whatever he wants to any organization or charity he likes. I get to give 10 percent from any money I earn and I am free to offer my time. He normally requests that I write a check to the Heart Association in memory of his father who passed away before we were married.

Since I don't work outside the home now, I seldom earn money. I have made a separate agreement with God about what he wants from me. I get a small allowance every week (what Ramsey calls "Blow Money") and I started tithing on that. Then I started giving more. And now I give nearly all of whatever is left in my wallet on Sunday. It is nearly always closer to 50 percent or more. I seldom count it, but I put it in an envelope with my name on it and put it in the offering. What amazes me most is that when the church sends its record of contributions, I am always blessed to see how much I have given. I never want for anything. I always have just enough to help someone in need. We are debt free and our bills are paid on time. We have a savings account that we make deposits in every pay period and we have a 401K that we maximize every year. I have more freedom and security than I could ever have imagined if I had battled with my husband on the legal requirement of tithing. God knows my heart wants to give more but I want to be an authentic example of a follower of Christ with my husband even more. To argue this principle would not honor God or my husband.

There are many behaviors stressed in Christian communities that will work in Christian homes that will not work in mine and perhaps not yours without leaning towards legalism. The music we listen to, the movies we choose, the food and drink we consume, and in what quantities are all potential booby traps for legalism. Talk to God about your situation, and ask His guidance for an authentic way to worship Him with your resources and choices without becoming legalistic. This alone will teach your husband indirectly that God cares more about our interaction with Him than He cares about well-meaning, mindless rule following. God will honor your obedience, your home will be peaceful, and your husband will love you for it.

Living in the Past. Being authentic with our husbands can be very challenging when we live in the past. There are times when all of us look back to times that were better. Sometimes when we reminisce, those memories may help us draw strength to get through a current crisis. A trip down memory lane, however, is far different than living in the past.

When we live in the past, we exhume old hurts and contaminate our own minds if we dwell on them; or worse yet, when we share those old hurts with others, we contaminate them. I am reminded of Genesis 19:26 "But Lot's wife looked back, and she became a pillar of salt."

One of my spiritually single friends discovered quite innocently from an e-mail her husband left on his computer screen that he was in a close e-mail relationship with another woman. She called him at work to let him know of her discovery. He said, "We need to talk when I get home from work." I have met more people who have been devastated by those words "We need to talk."

By the time he got home from work, she had played the scenario over in her mind a million times. Her worst suspicions were true. She caught her husband having an affair. He had tried to end it earlier. But it was truly over now. He was contrite. He was apologetic. She was devastated.

For the next several weeks and months, my friend realized that her husband's infidelity was her ticket out. She could divorce this man based on biblical principles and never look back. She sought God. I was honored she trusted my counsel. For months, we prayed through her numbness, her disgust, her anger, her rage, and her resolve. She decided to stay so her children would not be affected by his choices. She has never told her children or her parents of the pain she felt.

During the healing process, her husband bought her extravagant gifts. They went to counseling. They reframed their lifestyle and their style of communication. My friend's husband paid the price for his unfaithfulness every day in the form of his wife's distrust. He had to spend a long time re-earning her trust. For months, he disclosed his location with a call from his cell phone every time it changed. He gave her free reign to talk about their situation and her pain every time it bothered her.

Then one day, he simply said, "It's time to put this behind us. I love you and I want this to work. I can't change the mistake I made but I can no longer let it affect our future."

In that instant, my Christian friend had to make the decision to love, to look forward with her unsaved husband forever, or follow her hurt feelings. She ruminated in silence for a while, but she allowed God's love and influence to prevent her from becoming a pillar of salt in her own marriage.

Keeping it real can be very challenging. It can be filled with pain for a season. Also, there are barriers that can prevent us from becoming the conduit through which God's supernatural love flows to our husband. If we are aware of the barriers and decide to love, we prepare ourselves to have our gut reaction privately and our public reaction look and feel seamlessly loving.

The Next Wave

It is attention-grabbing to love the poor, to show compassion to AIDS sufferers, and to show mercy to victims. But it is attention-deflecting to wake up in the morning and ask, "What does my wife or husband, my daughter or son need?" and then attend to those needs. It is easier to see love in the public square than to show love in the home.

The Parable of the Good Samaritan is often misused here — as if love is shown only in the most extravagant of places, at the most unusual of times, and to the most needy of all persons. Not so, Jesus suggests: neighborly love begins in the home. In fact, if it is not shown in the home, it is a sham in public.[4]

Ten

Idolatry, Repentance, and Next Steps

I will bless you with a future filled with hope

— a future of success, not of suffering.

JEREMIAH 29:11

Contemporary English Version (CEV)

Idolatry

> *I am the Lord your God, who rescued you from the land of Egypt, the place of your slavery. You must not have any other god but me. You must not make for yourself an idol of any kind or an image of anything in the heavens or on the earth or in the sea.*
>
> *Exodus 20:2-4 NLT*

October 30th, 2009: I remember it so clearly. I sat down early in the morning after my husband left for work to spend some time alone with God before I drove across the Mojave Desert from San Diego to Phoenix. I had some real issues to talk to Him about and this morning's prayer time was really important. I was reading my Bible and getting myself prepared to pray when the phone rang. I stared down at the Caller ID to see — uh-oh! — my husband's office number clearly displayed. In a nanosecond, a million questions flashed through my mind: Auto accident on the way to work? Some news from the kids? What could he need so soon after he left home?

In that instant, I had a choice to make about who was first in my life: God or my husband? My final thought was "this will only take a moment and I can come back to God." I answered the phone. I had made my choice. I consciously chose my husband over God. I felt like Peter: "At that very moment, the last word hardly off his lips, a rooster crowed. Just then, the Master turned and looked at Peter. Peter remembered what the Master had said to him: 'Before the rooster crows, you will deny me three times.' He went out and cried and cried and cried."

I denied God my attention and my devotion and gave it instead to my husband. I wish I could say that my final thought "this will only take a moment and I can come back to God" was true. It was not. It did not take a moment. I could not come back to that quiet spot in the presence of God. I spent the next five hours putting out fires, re-arranging my schedule, and then starting my drive across the desert several hours later than I had planned.

I never got back to my pre-travel prayer, but as I heaved my things into the car and backed out of the driveway, I calmed down and asked God to forgive me. I knew that everything would have worked out so much differently, or at least I would have responded better, if I had just continued that special time in God's presence and returned the call to my husband.

And then I wondered as I drove, how many times I had denied Him? The Holy Spirit sent me memories of many times when I had worshiped my husband instead of Him. Unlike Peter, there were many more times than three; but, just like Peter, I cried and cried and cried. I was so saddened to have lost that opportunity with God and instead, be face-to-face with my own human-ness. The desert and me were both pretty dry that day.

My life has been a series of choices that started when I chose a man to be my husband with little regard for what God's word says. This has triggered a chain of decisions that often lead to compromises I wish I did not have to make. I ask God to keep me honest and of pure motives and this time my motives got checked.

Now before you begin examining times that you may have made choices that did not support your relationship with God, I want to caution you. The Holy Spirit is really good at this and He doesn't need you to dredge up the past. You will know when it happens, just like I did October 30, 2009. When the Holy Spirit shows you, you will cry. The real take away is this: God provides a way for us to find forgiveness through confession and repentance.

In 1 John 1:5-10, John says:

> *This is the message we have heard from him and declare to you: God is light; in him there is no darkness at all. If we claim to have fellowship with him yet walk in the darkness, we lie and do not live by the truth. But if we walk in the light, as he is in the light, we have fellowship with one another, and the blood of Jesus, his Son, purifies us from all sin. If we claim to be without sin, we deceive ourselves and the truth is not in us. If we confess our sins, he is faithful*

and just and will forgive us our sins and
purify us from all unrighteousness . If we
claim we have not sinned, we make him
out to be a liar and his word has no place
in our lives.

The first step is to confess, either alone in prayer with God, or with a prayer partner. It is this act of admitting that you did something wrong that brings God's forgiveness. If you are truly upset by the situation you are in, it may be best to ask another person to pray for you so that you can truly experience all of God's forgiveness and get it off your chest. Then take responsibility for what you did. This releases you from guilt and gives God's forgiveness a bigger space in your heart to cleanse.

The next step is to repent. This means to be truly sorry for what you did. True repentance means that you are so sorry for the sin you just committed that you never want to disappoint God with it again. You don't want to continue on in the same sin, you want a clean slate so you can be changed as you go forward.

The final step is to ask forgiveness for what you did and God is "faithful and just to forgive." We don't have to beg. He just forgives. He cleanses. He restores us to His original design rather than the distortion that we have created. In some instances, we may then have to go back to anyone we may have harmed with our sin and ask their forgiveness too.

I have had times when I had to repent alone for my actions and other times when I had to come to my husband and ask him to forgive me after I had already received God's forgiveness. He is clearly the more mature of the two of us and is always more readily forgiving than I would be.

But discretion is key here. Our husbands frequently will not have their radar up on sin like we do. On October 30, 2009, I did not have to go to my husband and ask his forgiveness because he was not even aware that he had interrupted my time alone with God. But on times when I have made a mistake that affects him (like the time I forgot a mortgage payment and we got a nasty note from the bank), it is important to ask his forgiveness. I prayerfully hope that my behavior provides him with a model for repentance that he will one day use in relationship with God.

Next Steps: My Story

I have been quite open throughout the pages of this book about my experience being married to a Jewish man. I have adopted certain behaviors that promote domestic peace in our home. My husband may not be adversarial to Jesus like some of the people in the Jewish faith and culture, but through his exposure to me he recognizes more Christian imagery now.

He is not comfortable with overt Christian symbols so I try to avoid having those types of things on display as to not offend him. For instance, I have never put up my Happy Birthday Jesus banner at Christmas, but I typically have a Christmas tree. I would love to wear a cross necklace and profess my love for and belief in Christ in ways that are recognized by others who believe as I do. But, I don't own a cross necklace. Overt Christian symbolism would distract my husband and diminish my primary purpose: to love and share the love, mercy, and grace of Christ with my husband and by extension, the Jewish culture he brings to our lives.

Instead, I wear a tiny crown on a chain around my neck that reminds me that I am a princess. Galatians 3:26-29 says:

> *You are all sons of God through faith in Christ Jesus, for all of you who were baptized into Christ have clothed yourselves with Christ. There is neither Jew nor Greek, slave nor free, male nor*

female, for you are all one in Christ Jesus. If you belong to Christ, then you are Abraham's seed, and heirs according to the promise.

I know my crown means that I am a princess, saved by the grace of Jesus from my mundane life and adopted in to royalty! God knows what it means to me and I would say he even inspired the thought of wearing the crown. Does it really matter if anyone else knows what it means?

I get a lot of questions about my crown and I am always happy to tell people that God considers me a princess because of the commitment I have made to love and serve him. Christians get it and even my Jewish family members find that answer acceptable. As other members of my family have made similar commitments, I bestow upon them their own crown necklace. It has become a little family subculture in our mission field.

Donna's Update

My friend Donna is married to Bill, a Muslim man from Turkey. Oftentimes, Donna and I share the progress we see in our husband's faith. Recently she wrote me an e-mail:

> *We had the most interesting conversation today. Bill and I were eating dinner and Cari, our teenage daughter, was sitting and talking with us about her school schedule for next year. She said she was considering a class on world religion. Cari expressed that there are so many different faiths, how could a person put so much faith in Christ? She*

wanted to explore the structure and foundations of other faiths.

Bill immediately said that there is only one religion that has a solid and indisputable base and it is Christianity and that base is Jesus. The whole world recognizes B.C. as before Christ and A.D. as after Christ. Christ had to have been more than a prophet like Muhammad was.

Bill went on to say that the teaching and morals that Christ tried to spread were the basis of humanity to help all people live together. Bill stated that from his religious training, he remembered Muhammad had 8 + wives under the age of 13; and, women in some Muslim cultures today are still stoned to death for minor infractions.

How can that teach world peace to its followers when people's lives (women who share the same faith) have no value?? ...WOW! What turns him away from Christianity is that so many hide under the blanket of Christianity and truly are not practicing their faith.

Please keep Bill in your prayers...he is in many ways more of a Christian than most people that claim to be. He does believe in Jesus, just not completely ...yet!

It is obvious to me that whatever Donna is doing, it's working. They are reaching a common ground in their faith. Through Donna's patient, loving example, Bill realizes that Jesus is more real and more important than Muhammad. He realizes the lifestyle that Muhammad led was not exemplary and the example he set has led specifically to difficulty for Muslim women. Bill has two daughters that are beautiful and brilliant. He wants them to have all the benefits a Christian lifestyle affords them that a Muslim lifestyle cannot.

What's Your Story?

Articulating my thoughts about my spiritually single lifestyle was an exceptionally helpful tool for growth. Many of us are so far into the lifestyle that we don't even realize we are in it. Just like the frog on the stove does not know the water temperature in the pan is rising until he is cooked, we swim through life without realizing that the temperature may have changed.

We get uncomfortable. We see and feel the effects but, like the frog, we are helpless to change. Unlike the frog, we have a God who wants us to be aware of our surroundings and be part of our lives. He wants to usher us from one road to the next and be an integral part of our journey. He wants to change us and use our change to impress, and ultimately save, our husbands.

Change happens. It is a fact of life. Fear of change, does not stop change. It only stunts our preparedness for the opportunity that change brings. How do we assess the change that has taken place around us so we know what to do?

I have created a questionnaire that I find quite helpful to articulate my feelings about the issues that surround being spiritually single. Some of the answers are static, but some have changed through the years as we move, as children leave the nest or reach lifetime milestones like salvation decisions, confirmations, baptisms, marriages, graduations, and parenthood.

I have mine tucked into my Bible and refer to it frequently (about as often as I move, but you may want to come up with a more suitable benchmark like your birthday or anniversary) to see if there is anything new that can be added.

Since I made the conscious decision to love my husband the way Jesus would, I can see the changes have happened for the better.

So start with the questionnaire first — it appears at the end of this chapter. Then take a moment to write your story. Share it with someone else who is spiritually single or share it with me. You can send it to: socalchris@gmail.com.

Call to Action

Consider the five things that Rick Warren says humans are hard wired to do in *The Purpose Driven Life:*

1. Worship (to God)
2. Fellowship (with believers)
3. Discipleship (learning from other Christians and then teaching others)
4. Ministry (to other believers)
5. Missions (to nonbelievers)

How are you going to incorporate those precepts (in this order) in your life as a spiritually single wife with little time to serve while you still please your husband who may not understand?

I encourage you to pray about leading or co-leading a small group of spiritually single women who, like you, need a place to belong and a group of female friends for mutual, spiritual support.

Give yourself a place to tell the story you create in this chapter. There is a Study Guide in the back of this book to guide you as well as a list of reading references that I recommend. There is also help on my website www.spirituallysinglewives.com and even more resources to draw from long after you have finished studying this book.

Questionnaire

1. I married my husband (before or after) becoming a Christian.

2. We dated for _____(length of time) before marrying.

3. My husband identifies with _____(which faith?).

4. As a follower of the above faith, on a scale of 0 to 5 (5 being the most) how ardent do you think he is in his faith? Using the same scale, how ardent does he believe himself to be?

5. Tell us what you know about his faith, his religion, and his culture. Share what his traditions have meant to you.

6. Was his family supportive of your courtship/marriage in the beginning? How did (do) they show their feelings about your cross-cultural relationship today?

7. Was God a subject that was brought up during your courtship? If so, tell what your discussions were about. Do you talk about God today? Is there a difference in your discussions now?

8. Do you perceive your difference in faith as a cultural or religious problem? How so?

9. How do his perspectives affect you?

10. How does your difference in faith affect your children?

11. Give the best example(s) of when you saw God at work in your life. In his life?

12. Do you have any joys or regrets to share because of the man you married and the differences between you and he?

13. If you had it all to do over again, would you still choose this man and live this life with him?

14. What would you share with another woman who might consider marriage outside her faith?

15. When you attend church, what one thing would you like others to know about your spiritually single situation?

The Next Wave

It is time for the body of Christ to realize that the Christian wife of an unbeliever is not a second-class citizen in the church. She is a woman whom God has called to a noble and difficult ministry. Wives of unbelievers must stop regarding themselves as failures incapable of getting their husbands saved and instead see themselves as selected saints chosen to represent Christ to their husbands in the most intimate of relationships — marriage. And it is time for us all to acknowledge that being the wife of an unsaved husband is not a sin but, in fact, an honorable calling.[1] How do you feel about this quote?

Recommended Reading for the Spiritually Single

Berry, Jo. Beloved *Unbeliever: Loving Your Husband Into the Faith*. Zondervan. 1981.

Black, Sabrina. *Can Two Walk Together? Encouragement for Spiritually Unbalanced Marriages.* Moody Press. 2002.

Eldredge, John. *Wild at Heart*. Thomas Nelson. 2001.

Kennedy, Nancy. *When He Doesn't Believe: Help and Encouragement for Women Who Feel Alone in Their Faith*. Waterbrook Press. 2001.

Odell, Jeri. *Spiritually Single; Living with an Unbelieving Husband*. Beacon Hill Press of Kansas City. 2002.

Schaeffer, Edith. *Christianity is Jewish*. Tyndale House Publishers, Inc. 1975.

Strobel, Lee and Leslie. *Surviving a Spiritual Mismatch*. Zondervan. 2002.

Thomas, Gary. *Sacred Influence*. Zondervan. 2006.

Thomas, Gary. *Sacred Marriage*. Zondervan. 2000.

Appendix: Study Guide

This guide is provided as a tool for leading a small group of spiritually single wives. There are other suggestions, exercises, and teaching tools available at www.spirituallysinglewives.com.

One

Spiritually Single

Welcome & Purpose

Welcome to Spiritually Single Wives, a small group for wives who are spiritually single — wives who share everything with their husband except their faith in Christ. The purpose of this group is to share the love, grace, and mercy of Christ Jesus with each other by sharing and bearing each other's burdens, expressing our love and care for one another, and encouraging one another. We do so to find peace, joy, and godliness in our marriages and ultimately find hope and purpose in God. And along the way, I hope we have some fun!

Opening Prayer

Heavenly Father, we pray that you join our group and be a part of each and every discussion we have. We invite the Holy Spirit to hover about this room and bring His tender mercies, His guidance, His forgiveness, and openhanded grace, then follow us home where He can work miracles in our families. We pray that you would mend hearts and minds and provide a caring and concerned nucleus here for women who love you without the spiritual support and encouragement of the men they love. Let us learn your way for our spiritually single lives. In Jesus' name, Amen.

Questions

1. Since the heart of a small group is interaction, take a moment to introduce yourselves to everyone. Share something unique about yourself with the group. Jot down a note or two as each member shares or make a simple seating chart to keep track of new names and faces. These faces may become important to you in ways you had never thought.

2. Spiritually speaking, what does your husband think of you?

Closing Prayer

Heavenly Father, we ask you to bless each of us at this beginning point. Help us remain committed to the work you are doing in each of us and through this small group. We thank you in advance for building lifetime bonds between us as we learn together your perspective on our spiritually single homes. Bless us as we leave today and bring us back to the next meeting with new insights to share. In Jesus' name, Amen.

Homework

Read Chapter Two "We Need Girlfriends" and be ready to discuss questions with the group.

Memory Verse

> *I will bless you with a future filled with hope—a future of success, not of suffering.*
>
> *Jeremiah 29:11*
> *Contemporary English Version (CEV)*

Two

We Need Girlfriends

Opening Prayer

Dear Lord: Thank you for this small group where we can know and be known by trustworthy female friends who will love us unconditionally. Let us find comfort and encouragement in our small group where we can learn more about you, how to be more like you, and then how to serve you. Thank you for these women who will pray for each other. Give us an extra measure of love for one another for the glory of your kingdom and the transformation of our families. In Jesus' name we pray, Amen.

Questions

1. Who is your best friend? Why?

2. Look around you? Who has God placed in your life that might become a spiritual support for you? Is there a Donna in your life?

3. Have you ever had a connection with a male friend that was difficult in your marriage? How did you solve that problem? (Author's note: If you have been fooled into sinning by the enemy, there is forgiveness and redemption for you. Confess your sin to God and receive his forgiveness. Then walk in repentance away from the sin.)

4. Warfare is always around us but sometimes it starts so subtly that we don't notice until we are so far into it that we are in danger. Could you share with the group a time when you realized you were experiencing spiritual warfare? If you told that same story to your husband, what would he have thought?

5. Often times, spiritually single wives feel isolated because they have one foot in the world and one

foot in the church. Can you share an experience when you felt that way?

6. Describe an experience when you shared something spiritual with your husband and he understood you. How did that make you feel? What did you do next?

7. Describe an experience when you shared something spiritual with your husband and you could tell he did not understand. How did that make you feel? What did you do next?

8. Have you developed a group of female friends that share or have empathy for your spiritually single condition? Recommend ways you have used to develop those friendships for others in the group who may not have gotten started.

9. Do you have a very best friend who prayerfully supports you? Describe how you met and how long you have been connected.

10. Could you become a mentor/femtor? Under what conditions? Formal or informal?

11. Write a want ad for the perfect best friend. Identify key characteristics of the mentor/femtor that would be best for you. Tuck these away in your Bible and see how God provides!

Closing Prayer

Heavenly Father, we ask you to lead us to a small group of women with whom we feel your divine connection. We pray to both find a mentor and, as you work in us, we grow to become one as well. We pray for a supernatural blessing that breaks down the shame and the social barriers we who are spiritually single often feel. Please provide us with at least one person in a similar situation that we can trust to give and receive support and encouragement. We pray this in Jesus' name, for our encouragement and your glory, Amen.

Homework

- Have every person at your small group sign in today and designate one person to compile the list and distribute it by e-mail. When the list arrives in your inbox, make a point this week to call the person below your name on the list just to ask how she is doing and if she has a prayer request. The last person should call the first person. Follow up with that person at the next meeting.

- Read Chapter Three "Our Behavior" and answer questions.

Memory Verse

> *As iron sharpens iron,*
>
> *so one [wo]man sharpens another.*
>
> *Proverbs 27:17*

Three

Our Behavior

Opening Prayer

Heavenly Father, we ask that as we examine the behavior we need to model in our homes that you work miracles in us. Make our behavior an outgrowth of a changed heart, mind, and perspective. Today, we ask you to open our minds and spirits so that you can change us to become the wives you intend us to be for our unsaved husbands. We trust you to bring us into a new level of awareness that will help us understand our husbands like you do. We love you Lord and we want to be more like you. In Jesus' name, Amen.

Questions

1. How do you feel about the words *purity* and *reverence?*

2. Of the four definitions of pure, which one do you most relate to? Why? Share how you use or plan to use this definition?

3. If your husband was given that definition of purity, would he tell others that he sees that in you?

4. Are you able, after seeing Sarah's submission, to better understand extending the grace of God to your husband? List two ways that you can submit now (or have done in the past) that would really surprise your husband.

5. Liken your life to a car. If others saw your life would they want to trade up to it? What features do you have that are sales points for your model? What features do you have that your husband likes? List two features you would like to add to your model?

6. Which of the four emotional challenges that were mentioned in this chapter affect you the most?

Stop now and confess to God your concerns and ask him to change you from the inside.

7. Have you ever gone somewhere or done something with your husband that you did not want to just because he wanted to? Tell the group about a time when your submission benefited you more than him.

8. Do you ever feel like you are too carnal for the church and too holy for the secular world? Jesus lived that way everyday of his short life on earth. By using his example, how does that make you feel?

9. Are you waiting for your husband to join you before you move forward in serving Christ? List two things you do now to serve God. Is God speaking to you about other areas of ministry?

Closing Prayer

Dear Lord, we pray that before we open our mouths to speak about you that we will demonstrate your grace and your goodness to the people we love the most — our husbands and family members. We pray for your forgiveness for any of the times our behavior was not befitting your name. Please cleanse us and rebuild us from the inside so that our purity and reverence shines through and appears effortless. Never let us get away with "acting" pure or reverent. Make us real and naked before you. Let our husbands see your transformation in our lives and be blessed by it. In Jesus' name, Amen.

Homework

▪ Ask your husband what it is like being married to you. Write his answer down and share it with the group.

▪ Read Chapter Four "The 'S' Word: Submission."

Memory Verse

Wives, in the same way be submissive to your husbands so that, if any of them do not believe the word, they may be won over without words by the behavior of their wives, when they see the purity and reverence of your lives.

1 Peter 3:1

Four

The "S" Word: Submission

Opening Prayer

Dear Lord, we pray that as we begin to study what submission is and what it is not, that you will give us your heart for the order that you have created for us as Christians, as wives and particularly as the wives of men who don't believe as we do. Let our actions and attitudes speak in our homes long before our words are made audible. We pray this in your name and for your glory, Amen.

Questions

1. How do you feel when you hear the word submission? (Be real!)

2. Does your husband usually make decisions in the best interest of your immediate family? Share an example.

3. Does your husband usually make decisions in your best interest? Share an example.

4. Does your husband usually consult you when making decisions that impact you and your family? Share an example.

5. Using one of the examples you gave above in Questions 2-4, share how your submission to your husband reflected God's design for your marriage.

6. How was Esther submissive?

7. What was her motive in not submitting to the king's rule (the rule about not approaching him without being summoned)?

8. What did she do before approaching him? And what did she risk? Do you think God could be preparing you as a spiritually single wife for "such a time as

this" when the salvation of your family is paramount?

9. Share a time when you did not submit to your husband. Did you see a chaotic period follow? Describe it for the group.

10. If submission is a gift we choose to give out of love, list two ways that you can lovingly submit to your husband today. List a third way: one that may not be genuine today that you can ask God to help you with.

Closing Prayer

Dear Lord, we pray that you will help us overcome our cultural bias toward the loving act of submission to our husbands so that we can bring your order to our homes and glory to your name. Bless us with the peace and contentment that comes from our obedience. Create in each of us an individual manner of purity that blesses our husbands and families uniquely.

Homework

Read Chapter Five "What A Man Wants."

Memory Verse

> Wives, submit to your husbands as to the Lord. For the husband is the head of the wife as Christ is the head of the church, His body, of which He is the Savior. Now as the church submits to Christ, so also wives should submit to their husbands in everything.
>
> Ephesians 5:22-24

Five

What a Man Wants

Opening Prayer

Dear God, we are learning that you designed our marriages with us in mind. We ask you to help us learn more about our husbands. No matter how many years we have known them, we realize that you, as their creator, know them better and are looking out for their best interest even more so than we are. Please have your way in our husbands' lives and let your love start with each of us. In Jesus' name, Amen.

Questions

1. What do you think your husband wants from you more than anything?

2. What are the three things a husband wants in a marriage? Rate yourself on a scale of 1 to 5 with 5 being the highest. How do you think you do on each of the three points?

3. Before the next meeting, ask your husband to rate you on the same scale. Tell the group what you learn about your relationship.

4. What part of respecting your husband is the easiest? What part is the most difficult? What can you do today to make the difficult part more doable?

5. Share any of the domestic arrangements that you and your husband have, either spoken or understood. How well do they work in your home? Are there some that need to be revisited now that you have been married for a while, added children, and/or made other life changes?

6. Are you and your husband on the same page sexually? What adjustments could be made so that both your needs can be met?

7. In Exodus 34:29-30: "When Moses came down from Mount Sinai with the two tablets of the Testimony in his hands, he was not aware that his face was radiant because he had spoken with the Lord. When Aaron and all the Israelites saw Moses, his face was radiant, and they were afraid to come near him." When I read this text I wondered, what do I radiate at my house? How about you? What do you radiate at your house?

8. Do you already have a special place and time devoted to God each day? Share with others in the group what you do, or ideas that you have that help you find time with God.

9. Why do you think it is important to take care of yourself first as a missionary in your own home?

Closing Prayer

Heavenly Father, if we have not been wives that our husbands could have full confidence in, please forgive us. Show us how to bring our husbands good in the ways they understand it best. We pray that you would give us your wisdom and compassion in our home mission field. We need time alone with you to confess our own issues and learn about your will and plan for internal change. Help us to accept our forgiveness and feel the power of your grace. Show us supernaturally how to forgive our husbands just like you forgive us and how to respect our husbands, provide them with domestic tranquility, and physical affection. Lord, let the transformation at home begin with us. In your name and for your glory on earth, and specifically our homes, we pray, Amen.

Homework

- Read Chapter Six "Set Apart: What Does Your Sanctification Mean to Him?"

- Remember: Before the next meeting, ask your husband to rate you on the same scale you used in this week's question number 2. Tell the group what you learned about your relationship.

- Choose one of the following for next week:

  1. If you have not already devoted a regular time and place to spend with God, make a plan and commit to one day this week, increasing as you become more comfortable in God's presence.

  2. Talk to your husband about your domestic arrangements and see if they are still working. Is it time for a modification?

  3. Silently invite God to be a part of your sex life. Don't tell your husband, keep it just between you and your Lord. Did you experience a change? Did your husband? Please, no reports to the group!!!

Memory Verse

Her husband has full confidence in her and lacks nothing of value. She brings him good, not harm, all the days of her life.

Proverbs 31:11-12

Six

Set Apart: What Does Your Sanctification Mean to Him?

Opening Prayer

Dear Lord, we are so grateful that you provide sanctification for our husbands through us. We pray that you would give us an extra measure of understanding for the complex almost cosmic connection that we have with our husbands and the implications that connection provides for us, our husbands, and our children. Let us see and cherish the sacred thread that we hold in our hands that ties our husbands to you. Thank you Lord for this calling, giving us the honor of sharing your love and holiness with our husbands in a unique and personal way. In Jesus' name we pray, Amen.

Questions

1. What does sanctification mean to spiritually single wives?

2. How much of your growth as a person, spiritually, mentally and/or emotionally can be attributed in some way to the partnership you share with your husband?

3. Review the definition of sanctify again. In what ways is your husband sanctified by your relationship with him?

4. 4.You, as a believer, are in a sanctification process. The outcome is holiness. How does holiness flesh out in your life? Is it something that your husband perceives as a good thing? Or does your holiness separate you from him? What are real and genuine ways for God's holiness in you to be positive for your husband?

5. How has your husband been set apart and used in your life to help you grow and become more Christ-like?

6. Have you ever considered divorce? What kept you from going through with it? Have you seen a transformation in yourself because you made the commitment to stay? If you have been divorced, share what you have learned from God since then.

7. Have you ever thought about spiritual warfare like a strategic battle of good vs. evil? If you lose the battle, what happens? Share ways you know from personal experience that help you win in that ongoing battle.

8. Do you see a sense of the profane in your husband that just does not fit with "church culture?" Remembering that your group has a confidentiality agreement, share with the group your experience with the profane at your home.

9. Tell the group about a time when you supported your husband in a way that might have been judged by others and found that God lives out in the world too.

10. Have you seen any "blighted things" appearing in the place of fruit at your house?

11. In an earlier chapter, we discussed the importance of girlfriends. Reflect on this chapter's discussion of the profane. Share your ideas about the importance of fellowship with other spiritually single women now.

12. Individually now, and later as a group during your group fellowship time, pray for God to quicken the heart of our churches and provide inspirational, culturally relevant, and creative ways to welcome the unchurched and bridge the gap between them and our heavenly Father.

Homework

- Read Chapter Seven "What About My Children?"

- Watch The Passion of the Christ. Give your honest response to what you saw in the film in regard to God's love for your husband. Share how that perspective changes you.

Memory Verse

> *For the unbelieving husband has been sanctified through his wife, and the unbelieving wife has been sanctified through her believing husband. Otherwise your children would be unclean, but as it is, they are holy. But if the unbeliever leaves, let him do so. A believing man or woman is not bound in such circumstances; God has called us to live in peace. How do you know, wife, whether you will save your husband? Or, how do you know, husband, whether you will save your wife?*
>
> *1 Corinthians 7:14-16*

Seven

What About My Children?

Opening Prayer

Dear Lord, we are so humbled and honored to be the guardians of your children. You are the Heavenly Father of our children and we know that what you have in store for them far surpasses our prayers, hopes, and dreams. We pray that you will give us the ability to be godly role models for our children and that as they grow up, they will be your messengers to the unsaved of the world — especially their dads. We pray that your protection be upon each of our children until their dads accept their role as spiritual leaders in our home. More than anything, we pray that our kids learn to grow in your love and admonition and find their purpose in God's kingdom. In Jesus' name, Amen.

Questions

1. Are your kids able to understand and/or see the difference in faith between you and your husband? If so, how does that affect them?

2. Can you identify when your children became a catalyst for change in your life? How did that affect your relationship with God? With your husband?

3. The section titled "The End Game" could be rewritten for each family. After reading this section, rewrite "The End Game" and personalize it for your own children. Be specific.

4. What are some of the values you would like to instill in your children? Do you and your husband agree on these things? What can both of you agree on?

5. If values are caught, not taught, what concerns you about the values your children are learning from you? From your husband?

6. Describe a time of spiritual friction in your home and discuss what happened. If the same friction reared its ugly head again, how would you cope differently with it now?

7. Do you often have issues on Sunday getting to church with your kids? What might take some of the pressure off?

8. Have you ever felt like you were responding to your children out of a rigid set of rules instead of love and guidance? What rules are your pitfalls? Do you ever check yourself on that? How?

9. Describe the ground rules you and your husband use, either assumed or previously discussed, and how they are working for you. Is it time to have a discussion with your husband about modifying or adding some rules as your children grow older? What would you like to change?

10. How have your children's milestones affected your husband? As they grow spiritually do you see the benefit of preparing your husband for their spiritual milestones? How will you do that?

11. Have a private discussion with your husband about some of the questions you both need to be prepared to answer. If appropriate, share the results of your conversation with the group.

Homework

- After you have finished question number 3 from this week's study, discuss it with your husband if possible and see if he agrees with the direction you are headed with each of your children.

- Read Chapter Eight "Rapport: Finding Common Ground."

Memory Verse

Train up a child in the way he should go: and when he is old, he will not depart from it.

Proverbs 22:6

Eight

Rapport: Finding Common Ground

Opening Prayer

Dear Lord, you already know that as spiritually single wives, our lifestyles are made up of a series of compromises. We pray that you will send your Holy Spirit to help us see how to best avoid opportunities to sin without pointing fingers of judgment. Teach us to accept whatever tools you give us — even if they may appear secular — to nurture our husbands in the process of their salvation. Teach us to reframe our communication in such a way that our husbands can learn more about our value system in Christ. Bless us with a blueprint to build rapport with our husbands so that we can love them as you do. We pray all this in your name, for your glory, and for the salvation of our husbands, Amen.

Questions

1. When you hear the word secular, what does it mean to you?

2. Using the definition provided for secularism, "to order and interpret life based on principles taken solely from this world without recourse to a belief in God and future life," describe the dangers you see of secularism in the church.

3. Do you see a measure of secularism in your husband's approach to life? Share how you integrate his secularism in your marriage, home, and family.

4. What battles do you have in your marriage that might be better understood if they were reframed in a secular viewpoint?

5. List the top three values in your home and explain how you and your husband make them work. Ask

your husband what his top three values are and see if your perspective matches his.

6. Veni, vidi, vici. We came, we saw, we conquered. If there were three words on your family crest, what would they be? For fun, look them up on igoogle.com and translate those three words in a language that is meaningful to you. Then draw a family crest.

7. How can you use the information from question 5 to build rapport with your husband?

8. There are seventeen values identified in Proverbs 31. As you look at them, put a "+" sign next to the three that are your strengths. Put a "-" next to the three that are your weaknesses.

9. Of those seventeen values, place a "*" next to the three values you think your husband would like to see you aspire to. What steps can you take to get started? Ask your husband for suggestions.

10. List a few things you do now to bless your husband. Has that changed significantly since you first married? Do you think the changes please or displease your husband? How?

Homework

Read Chapter Nine "Keep It Real."

Memory Verse

Respect what is right in the sight of all men. If possible, so far as it depends on you, be at peace with all men.

Romans 12:17-18

Nine

Keep It Real

Opening Prayer

Heavenly Father, we pray that you would give us the courage to live and love authentically. Overwhelm us with your grace so that we can extend it to the ones that are closest to us. Show us the most effective ways to love our husbands. Bring us resources to share that might bring our husbands a step closer to you. Help us discern between your principles and the cultural ideologies that create obstacles for our husbands in their faith. We pray all this in your name, Amen.

Questions

1. Are you still magically in love with your husband? What one thing could you do to improve your relationship?

2. List your husband's favorite love language(s). List yours. How do you make those languages work in your marriage?

3. Has your husband ever had a reaction to an experience that led you to believe your behavior was having an effect on him spiritually?

4. Have well-meaning Christians ever made judgmental remarks in front of or about your husband? What was his reaction? How did you respond?

5. Has your husband ever accused you of being a hypocrite? How did that make you feel?

6. Do you have a strategy for reducing hypocrisy in your relationship?

7. As Christian women, we identify role models at church that we admire and aspire to become. We forget that as our value system changes, our

husbands don't share this experience and their value system remains unchanged. Have you ever been called self-righteous?

8. What area(s) in your marriage have become fragile because you have brought in church values that your husband was unwilling or unable to embrace?

9. Does your husband know about your personal devotional time? Is he supportive? Is he critical?

10. Are there any issues over which you and your husband disagree? Is there a way to reach out to your husband by using training material that has Christian content?

11. Describe a particular time in your life that was destructive to your walk with Christ or the health of your marriage, what would that be? Confess that to the group, or if it is too private, seek out a mentor to share your experience. Allow God to forgive you and cleanse you from the past. Receive His forgiveness and move forward in repentance (turning away from the sin).

12. As you look at the situations that can sabotage the authenticity in your relationship with your husband — hypocrisy, self-righteousness, legalism, and living in the past — which one causes you to stumble the most? How will you try to resolve that, not by wordy proclamations, but silently through your behavior?

Homework

Read Chapter Ten "Idolatry, Repentance, and Next Steps."

Memory Verse

If I speak in the tongues of men and of angels, but have not love, I am only a resounding gong or a clanging cymbal.

1 Corinthians 13:1

Ten

Idolatry, Repentance, and Next Steps

Opening Prayer

Heavenly Father, as we come together for the last chapter of this book, we pray that you be with us today as we seek to learn from you and to honor you with what we have learned. In Jesus' Name, Amen.

Questions

1.What's your story? Be prepared to share it with your small group.

2. Discuss the results of the questionnaire on page 115.

Closing Prayer

Dear God, I pray that each woman who reads this workbook and answers these questions absorbs just the information that you and the Holy Spirit find important for her today. Bless each woman with an overarching concern for the salvation of her husband and an awareness of the awesome privilege and responsibility for which you have gifted her in her mission: to love her husband with the love of Christ. I pray that today, each woman walks away with a connection to a friend or a larger group that helps meet her need for spiritual intimacy and acceptance in the body of Christ. Help each woman determine her way to serve you meaningfully that does not conflict with her husband's expectations. As they go on their journeys, I pray that the Holy Spirit will envelope them with protection and comfort. We pray for your change in each of their homes. Let them be the branch on the family tree that changes the family history forever.

Memory Verse

I will bless you with a future filled with hope — a future of success, not of suffering.

Jeremiah 29:11

Contemporary English Version (CEV)

End Notes

It should be noted that, unless specified in the text, all scripture quoted is taken from the New International Version Holy Bible. New International Version ® Copyright © 1973, 1978, 1984 International Bible Society.

One
Spiritually Single
1. Berry, Jo. *Beloved Unbeliever: Loving Your Husband into the Faith*. Grand Rapids, MI: Zondervan, 1981, pp. 108-109.

Two
We Need Girlfriends
1. Strobel, Lee and Leslie. *Surviving a Spiritual Mismatch in Marriage*. Grand Rapids, MI: Zondervan, 2002, p. 74.

Three
Our Behavior
1. *purity*. (2010). In *Merriam-Webster Online Dictionary*. Retrieved April 26, 2010 from http://www.merriam-webster.com/dictionary/pure.

2. *pure*. (2010). In *Merriam-Webster Online Dictionary*. Retrieved April 26, 2010 from http://www.merriam-webster.com/dictionary/pure.

3. *reverence*. (2010). In *Merriam-Webster Online Dictionary*. Retrieved April 26, 2010 from http://www.merriam-webster.com/dictionary/reverence.

4. Strobel, Lee and Leslie. *Surviving a Spiritual Mismatch in Marriage*. Grand Rapids, MI: Zondervan, 2002, p. 130.

5. *The IVP New Testament Commentary Series, Vol. 3: Luke*. Downer's Grove, IL: InterVarsity Press, 1994.

6. Strobel, Lee and Leslie. *Surviving a Spiritual Mismatch in Marriage*. Grand Rapids, MI: Zondervan, 2002, p. 118.

Four

The "S" Word: Submission

1. *submission*. (2010). In Merriam-Webster Online Dictionary. Retrieved April 26, 2010 from http://merriam-webster.com/dictionary/submit.

2. Chapman, Gary. *The Five Love Languages: How to Express Heartfelt Commitment to Your Mate*. Chicago, IL: Northfield Publishing, p. 140.

Five

What A Man Wants

1. Adapted from a talk given by Tom Shrader of East Valley Bible Church, Gilbert, AZ, 2001.

2. Strobel, Lee and Leslie. *Surviving a Spiritual Mismatch in Marriage*. Grand Rapids, MI: Zondervan, 2002, p. 104.

3. Omartian, Stormie. *The Power of a Praying Wife*. Eugene, OR: Harvest House Publishers, 1997, p. 64.

4. Warren, Rick. *The Purpose Driven Life: What on Earth Am I Here For?* Grand Rapids, MI: Zondervan, 2002, p. 89.

5. Warren, Rick. *The Purpose Driven Life: What on Earth Am I Here For?* Grand Rapids, MI: Zondervan, 2002, p. 306.

6. Milne, A.A. *The House at Pooh Corner*. Penguin Books, USA, 1992, p. 120.

Six
Set Apart: What Does Your Sanctification Mean to Him?

1. *sanctify*. In *Merriam-Webster Online Dictionary*. Retrieved May 19, 2010 from http://www.merriam-webster.com/dictionary/sanctify.

2. *sanctification*. *Baker's Evangelical Dictionary of Biblical Theology*. Edited by Walter A. Elwell. Copyright 1996. Baker Books, Grand Rapids, MI http://www.biblestudytools.com/dictionaries/bakers-evangelical-dictionary/sanctification.html.

3. *holy*. *Baker's Evangelical Dictionary of Biblical Theology*. Edited by Walter A. Elwell. Copyright 1996. Baker Books, Grand Rapids, MI http://www.biblestudytools.com/dictionaries/bakers-evangelical-dictionary/sanctification.html.

4. Lewis, C.S. *The Screwtape Letters*, San Francisco, CA: Harper San Francisco, New Edition, 2001.

5. Schaeffer, Edith. *Christianity is Jewish*. Huemoz, Switzerland: L'Abri Fellowship, 1975, pp. 169-170.

6. Schaeffer, Edith. *Christianity is Jewish*. Huemoz, Switzerland: L'Abri Fellowship, 1975, pp. 169-170.

7. Kennedy, Nancy. *Between Two Loves: Devotions for Women Whose Husbands Don't Share Their Faith*. Grand Rapids, MI: Zondervan, 2003, p. 45.

Seven
What About My Children?
1. Strobel, Lee and Leslie. *Surviving a Spiritual Mismatch in Marriage*. Grand Rapids, MI: Zondervan, 2002, pp. 109-110.

2. Campbell, Joseph. *The Hero with a Thousand Faces*. New York: Princeton University Press, 1949,1968, 1972, 1973, p. 4.

3. Strobel, Lee and Leslie. *Surviving a Spiritual Mismatch in Marriage*. Grand Rapids, MI: Zondervan, 2002, p. 110.

4. Strobel, Lee and Leslie. *Surviving a Spiritual Mismatch in Marriage*. Grand Rapids, MI: Zondervan, 2002, p. 112.

5. Strobel, Lee and Leslie. *Surviving a Spiritual Mismatch in Marriage*. Grand Rapids, MI: Zondervan, 2002, p. 108.

6. Kennedy, Nancy. *Between Two Loves: Devotions for Women Whose Husbands Don't Share Their Faith*. Grand Rapids, MI: Zondervan, 2003, p. 139.

Eight
Rapport: Finding Common Ground
1. *secular*. Edited by F.L. Cross and E. A. Livingstone. *Oxford Concise Dictionary of the Christian Church*. Oxford, England: Oxford University Press, 1974, p. 1255.

2. Williamson, Marianne. *Return to Love: Reflections on the Principles of A Course in Miracles*. New York, NY: Harper Perennial, 1992, p. 191.

3. Miller, Donald. *Blue Like Jazz*. Nashville, TN: Thomas Nelson, Inc. 2003, p. 221.

Nine
Keep It Real
1. Chapman, Gary. *The Five Love Languages: How to Express Heartfelt Commitment to Your Mate*. Chicago, IL: Northfield Publishing, 1992, p. 38.

2. *legalism*. In *Merriam-Webster Online Dictionary*. Retrieved May 26, 2010 from http://www.merriam-webster.com/dictionary/legalism.

3. Ramsey, Dave. *The Total Money Makeover: A Proven Plan for Financial Fitness*. Nashville, TN: Thomas Nelson, Inc., 2003 (Recommended Percentages in Appendix).

4. McKnight, Scot. *The Jesus Creed: Loving God, Loving Others*. Brewster, MA: Paraclete Press, 2004, pp. 55-56.

Ten
Idolatry, Repentance, and Next Steps
1. Davis, Linda. *How to Be the Happy Wife of an Unsaved Husband*. New Kensington, PA: Whitaker House, 1987, p. 1.

7658763R0

Made in the USA
Charleston, SC
28 March 2011